THE WORLD OF SAN MIGUEL DE ALLENDE
An Uncommon Guide

Robert de Gast

E&R Publications
San Miguel de Allende, Gto., Mexico

To Evelyn, with love.

Copyright © 2009 by Robert de Gast

All rights reserved. No part of this book may be reproduced or transmitted in any form or by any means, electronic or mechanical, including photocopying, recording or by any information storage and retrieval system, without permission in writing from the copyright holder.

ISBN 978-0-9655420-1-2
First Edition
Published by E&R PUBLICATIONS
Balcón de la Cañada 13
San Miguel de Allende, Gto.
Mexico 37790
443-321-8727 (USA)
415-152-7396 (MEX)
www.robertdegast.com

Designed and produced by Héctor Ulloa
Printed in Mexico

Contents

An Introduction to a Dusty Hillside Town	1
A Short History of a Long Time	9
The Historic District	47
Two Short Walks around Town	51
Other Interesting Sights	83
Barrios, Colonias, and *Fraccionamientos*	93
On Getting Around…	95
Street Names	99
House Numbers	109
More than Four Dozen Fountains	113
A Hundred Bells and Other Sounds…	117
A Miscellany of Doors and Door Knockers	121
Some Notables	125
Interesting Places a Little Farther Away	143
El Tianguis, the Tuesday Market	145
The Botanical Garden, El Charco del Ingenio	147
The Chapel at San Miguel Viejo	151
The *Presas*… Reservoirs	153
The Pyramid and Sanctuary at La Cañada de la Virgen	155
The Big Tree at La Huerta	156
A Few Hot Springs and a Cool Pool	157
Indian Chapels in the *Campo*	159
The Sanctuary of Atotonilco	161
Dolores Hidalgo, Cradle of Independence	163
The City of Santiago de Querétaro	165
The Abandoned Mining Town of Mineral de Pozos	167
Guanajuato, Hill of the Frogs	169
A Calendar of Events	171
Acknowledgments	215

An Introduction to a Dusty Hillside Town

There are more than 130 places called San Miguel in Mexico; the range is from A—Z: There is San Miguel Abejones in the state of Oaxaca, and San Miguel Zuapan, in the state of Puebla. For many people, though, San Miguel is San Miguel de Allende, a beautiful small town in the middle of Mexico that has become a world-class destination for tourists and retirees. (San Miguel de Allende's name is usually followed by the abbreviation for the state of Guanajuato, "Gto." There's another San Miguel de Allende, a mountain village with a population of about 300 in the state of Durango, and thus is written San Miguel de Allende, Dgo.) At various times there have been other names for the city: first, San Miguel de los Chichimecas or sometimes San Miguel de los Otomís, after Indian tribes; Villa de San Miguel, when officially recognized as a "Spanish" town; San Miguel el Grande, as the town grew in importance; and finally, in 1826, San Miguel de Allende, after Ignacio Allende, the city's great War of Independence hero.

San Miguel de Allende is located near the geographic center of Mexico at the edge of Mexico's breadbasket, known as *El Bajío* (The Lowlands), even though its altitude is around 6,000 feet. It is low compared to the ranges that flank it: the *Sierra Madre Oriental* and the *Sierra Madre Occidental*. The highest point is 2,750 meters (9,025 feet), found in *Los Picachos*, the mountain range a few miles south of San Miguel. Two extinct volcanoes, Palo Huérfano and La Joya, located in the range, last erupted about eight million years ago and volcanologists appear not to be worried. Mexico City is 180 miles south, the Texas border about 600 miles north. The area to the west, toward the *Sierra de Guanajuato*, 40 miles away, is mostly eroded due to deforestation. The area to the north is relatively flat, while much of the eastern flank is very flat, with large farms. The Bajío contains some of the most fertile agricultural land in the country. Only about ten percent of Mexico's land area can be used for agricultural purposes.

The state of Guanajuato has a population of about 5 million people, spread throughout 46 *municipios*. San Miguel de Allende is one of the largest of these counties, with an area of about 600 square miles, approximately half the size of Rhode Island. Ten percent of the state is covered by forests, 30 percent is used for agriculture (with 10 percent using irrigation), another 30 percent is considered "natural," while 20 percent of the state's area is completely eroded.

San Miguel is 600 miles from the nearest beach, has no airport, no casino, and at this writing, only one nine-hole golf course. But it also has no neon signs and only two traffic lights. Much of the architecture in the center of the city dates from the 18th century. Many of the streets are cobblestoned. All of the  sidewalks are narrow. Although designed as a grid-patterned town, not one block is entirely straight. While in Paris, a visitor might look ahead at the vistas or, in New York, look up at the buildings; in San Miguel you have to be looking down, negotiating the uneven streets and sidewalks. But it is not an altogether disagreeable task: much beauty is even to be found underneath one's feet.

Somebody once wrote, "If you combine the heavenly talents of St. Michael, the first among archangels, with the earthly skills of a Mexican War of Independence hero, you get San Miguel de Allende." Well, maybe, but you can't leave out the artists. What has made San Miguel de Allende one of the most popular travel destinations and retirement communities for Americans and Canadians in the last half century has precisely been its involvement with the arts. Anita Brenner, in her popular 1947 guide "Your Mexican Holiday," devoted only half a page on San Miguel, but wrote, "Not often visited by tourists, yet it is one of the loveliest classic colonial towns in Mexico… Because the whole town is virtually a museum piece, Mexican artists have founded a school for painters here." She recommended the town for honeymooners ("a jewel of a town… there are many who say this is the true fountain of youth"). Perhaps for the first time San Miguel de Allende was referred to in print as "an artistic center."

Dozens of art galleries are scattered around town. It wasn't always like this. The first one, the Galería San Miguel, opened in 1962 on the west side of the Jardín under the Portal Allende. It kept company with the first bookstore, El Colibrí and the first bar, La Cucaracha. Nearly half a century later the gallery is still in business, still on the plaza, now on the north side. The bookstore is gone, as is the bar. But there are now  several other galleries, almost all located in Centro or at the Fábrica La Aurora Art and Design Center.

Writing in the 1930s, when San Miguel was virtually abandoned, and many of the buildings nearly in ruins, the historian Francisco de la Maza, had this to say about the town's civil architecture:

> *The architectural landscape of the village, always harmonious and noble, has a shade of aristocracy and a sober elegance that bigger or more famous cities would like to have. … Tile and carved stone niches, crosses in corners and doorways, and coats of arms compete with the ancient gratings in balconies and the strength of their doors framed by carved jambs and high lintels. Houses that go up the hill and down to the meadows, curving in all directions, creating charming alleys and small plazas, and unimaginable recesses. Streets that climb in an arrogant slope following the trail of the singing water that runs down, leaping among the cobblestones of yesteryear. And it is all full of history. There is almost no street, house, corner or doorway that does not remind of a historical moment, the passing of an illustrious man, a birth, a death, a legend. … Stone by stone, they are felt, warmed by the hand of man."*

Much has been written about San Miguel's religious architecture. "Mexican churches," wrote Alice Adams, "so often have that slightly lopsided, mildly deranged look; they were clearly made by striving, imperfect, talented, but fallible human beings, which may account for some of their strong appeal... Churches, everywhere churches... San Miguel abounds in churches, all interesting and many quite beautiful." There are more than 300 in the munipicio, more than 20 in town.

And then there is the weather. Some of the words most often used to describe San Miguel's weather are "flawless," "perfect," and "wonderful." It is never extremely hot or terribly cold. Residents like to say that every day has four seasons: winter at dawn, spring in late morning, summer in the afternoon, and fall in the evening. The climate is temperate and the weather dry most of the year. The rainy season, from June to October, brings gentle, short showers several times a week in late afternoon, although occasionally heavy downpours occur during thunderstorms. But these also do not last very long. The rest of the year is not entirely without rain, but the amount and frequency of rainfall is extremely low.

There are no hurricanes. There are no tornadoes. There are no floods or wildfires. It doesn't snow. Frosts are extremely rare. During the warmest months, April and May, average low and high temperatures range from 54 to 83 degrees F (12 to 28 degrees C). In the coldest months, December and January, the average low and high temperatures range from 45 to 74 degrees F (17 to 23 degrees C). There can be, however, some spikes in those temperatures: afternoon temperatures in May can reach the low 90s, although humidity remains low. During December through February, early morning temperatures can hover for a few hours in the low 30s or 40s. These temperatures quickly soar because the sun shines seven hours a day on average, about 2,500 hours a year.

Air-conditioning is almost unknown, central heating rare. Comfort outdoors is regulated by layered clothing and walking on the sunny (or shady) side of the street.

The average year-round temperature is 66 degrees F (18.7 C) The average annual rainfall is about 25 inches (635mm). The average relative humidity is 67 percent. The average wind speed is 2.1 mph (3.4 km/h). The average descriptive word for all this is "spring-like."

Month	Temp. F max-min	Temp. C max-min	Rain/ inches	Rain/ mm
January	71/45	22/7	0.5	13
February	74/49	23/9	0.1	3
March	78/52	25/11	0.2	5
April	82/54	28/12	0.8	20
May	83/57	28/14	1.2	30
June	79/58	26/14	5.1	129
July	76/56	24/13	4.7	119
August	77/55	25/13	4.6	117
September	75/57	24/14	4.7	119
October	75/54	24/12	1.7	43
November	73/49	23/9	0.6	15
December	70/46	21/8	0.4	10

The opportunities in San Miguel for learning are astounding. A recent classified ad section in the English language newspaper *Atención* yielded the following subjects for which classes were being offered:

Aerobics, Acting, Art, Astrology, Bead Making, Belly Dance, Bridge, Ceramics, Cooking, Computer, Creative Writing, Dance, Dog Training, Drawing, Dressage, Feng Shui, French, German, Guitar, Japanese, Jewelry, Mask Making, Painting, Paper Making, Papier Mâché, Photography, Piano, Pilates, Quilting, Screenwriting, Sculpture, Singing, Spanish, Tango, Tennis, Watercolors, and Yoga.

There are many charitable organizations in San Miguel and many of the foreigners who have come to live in this town are involved in some form of community service. The aims and activities of these organizations range from protection for orphans or animals and the elderly, to medical care and scholarships for Mexican children.

San Miguel is renowned for its craftsmen. Much of the population is involved in producing various kinds of crafts. Metal workers, for example, produce objects in silver, brass, bronze, pewter, copper, and wrought iron. Furniture, rugs, and leather products are produced, as is blown glass, papier mâché, and embroidery. Stone carving and straw weaving remain some of the oldest skills least changed by time.

Casually sophisticated, intellectually stimulating and architecturally beautiful, San Miguel de Allende attracts thousands of Mexican and foreign visitors each year, and some stay (foreign residents account for about five percent of the population, around 5,000, with 70 percent from the U.S., 20 percent from Canada, and the rest from about 30 other countries). The population of Mexico in 40 years increased from about 34 million in 1960 to triple to more than 100 million by the year 2000.

At the end of the first decade of the 21st century the population stood at about 150,000 for the municipio, with about half of the inhabitants living in the urban area and half living in more than 500 rural communities, most with fewer than 300 inhabitants.

In 2008 San Miguel (and the nearby Santuario de Atotonilco) received the coveted UNESCO World Heritage Site designation and the city began to prepare for the much-anticipated celebrations in 2010 of the Bicentennial of the War of Independence and the Centennial of the 1910 Revolution.

The following pages will explore in words and pictures many interesting aspects of this colonial jewel, beginning with a short history and ending with a lengthy "Calendar of Events" listing the astonishing number and variety of fiestas that are celebrated in this "dusty, hillside town." As Octavio Paz, Mexico's Nobel laureate, wrote, "Fiestas are our luxury. … "

A Short History of a Long Time

The land surrounding today's San Miguel has seen human activity for thousands of years. Before the arrival of the Spaniards, the area, mostly forested, was inhabited by hunters-gatherers. These nomads, although generally called *Chichimecas*, were ethnically distinct tribes, such as *Cazcanes, Guamares, Copuces,* and *Guachichiles.*

The roving activities of the various Indian tribes brought a change in the culture and population of the *Bajío* (Lowlands), the fertile 5,000-6,000 foot high plateau that straddles the states of Guanajuato and Querétaro. In the early centuries of the Christian era this area had been settled by Indian tribes that practiced agriculture, the cultivation of corn and wheat in particular. Much unearthed pottery attests to their artistic and technical skills.

The majority of the archeological remains found around San Miguel de Allende were constructed between the years 950 and 1100 A.D. More than 100 archeological sites have been catalogued in the *municipio*. Most are small, except for the pyramid called *La Cañada de la Virgen*. (See The Pyramid, page 155.) The builders were allied to the political spheres of the Toltec Empire, but after about 1100 A.D., the Toltec civilization declined. Whether due to climate change or political realignment remains a contentious argument among archeologists and historians. In less than 100 years, the land was left desolate. After the year 1200, nomadic groups moved into the area. For more than 300 years, until the arrival of the Spaniards in the third decade of the 16th century, there had been no permanent settlements. These tribes did not farm but collected fruits, roots, and edible plants and hunted deer, boar, and other animals.

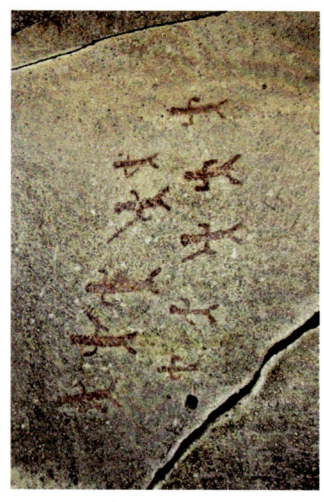

In the 1540s, less than two decades after the Conquest, Spaniards had begun moving north from central Mexico into the unexplored regions. The conquistadores came in search of riches, the clergy in search of souls to convert. The Spaniards called the area *tierra adentro* (inland) or sometimes *la frontera de los Chichimecas* (the frontier of the Chichimecas). The word Chichimeca is variously translated as "dog people," or "fur wearers," perhaps a pre-Columbian insult referring to their lack of woven clothes. More loosely it seems to mean nomads, barbarians, or savages. Around 1540 (the exact date is unknown, although 1542 is traditionally accepted), a barefoot Franciscan friar named Juan de San Miguel (see Notables, page 135), accompanied by a number of pacified and converted Tlaxcalteca, Tarascan and Otomí Indians, made his way north from Acámbaro, where the friar had served as Guardian of the Franciscan Monastery. They followed the Lerma River for about 60 miles until they found an agreeable site on the banks of a tributary to the Lerma, which they named the Río San Miguel (now Río Laja), and began to settle a small community. A chapel was fashioned out of tree branches and crude huts were built. It came to be known as San Miguel de los Chichimecas, named for the marauding tribes Fray Juan was to convert. After a short time he continued north on his evangelizing mission, leaving a French Franciscan friar, Bernardo Cossin, in charge of the small mission. (The site, now called San Miguel Viejo, is a few miles west of today's San Miguel de Allende.) Undefended and indefensible, the mission was vulnerable to attack by the Indians, who eventually struck. Historians disagree about when the settlement was attacked (1548? 1551?) and whether the Indians were Copuces or Guacamares. In any case, the attack left more than a dozen people dead and led to the temporary abandonment of the mission.

After the destruction of the first settlement, Fray Bernardo Cossin decided to find a more easily defendable place for the growing mission. A few miles up the slope of a hill called the Hill of Moctezuma was a copious spring, a *manantial*, later named *El Chorro* (The Spurt or Jet) that offered a more reliable water supply than the Río San Miguel and certainly a greater defensive position than the flat plain next to the river. A local legend insists that some dogs found the springs. The spot is still referred to as *Izquinapan*, (River of Dogs, from the Náhuatl "*izcuintli*" meaning "dog" and "*apan*" meaning "river"). A small chapel was built or a cross erected, but the steep site of El Chorro was inappropriate for a growing settlement. A more level area was selected for the layout of the town that, like the original settlement on the river, was called San Miguel. Fray Cossin eventually also kept moving north to continue his mission. He died in 1554, apparently at the hand of Indians.

In the late 1540s and 1550s more Spaniards and Indians came to live in the area. The former received grants of pasture lands to raise cattle or land for orchards with the obligation to care for and occupy the lands at least eight months of the year. They were forbidden to sell any part of the property for a period of five years.

The process of colonization accelerated after the discovery of silver in Zacatecas (250 miles north of San Miguel) and Guanajuato (40 miles west), setting off a rush into the still mostly unexplored northern territories. Within a few years mining camps appeared in many locations, although bellicose Chichimeca warriors made supplying the camps difficult and dangerous. By 1550 there were 34 mining companies in operation in Zacatecas and there was a well-traveled wagon trail between Zacatecas and Mexico City.

The historian David Frye, in his "Indians into Mexicans," described the growing problems between the Chichimecas and the Spaniards:

> *Nomads from across the northeast were drawn to a growing traffic of mule trains and caravans that supplied food and clothing to the fabulous mines of Zacatecas (discovered in 1546) and Guanajuato (1552), returning to Mexico City laden with silver. Deadly nomadic raids of the silver highway were countered by underpaid Spanish soldiers who sought their fortunes, or just made ends meet, by captur-*

*ing and enslaving entire bands of "wild Indians." Paying little regard to whether their captives had personally taken part in the warfare, the soldiers succeeded only in provoking retaliatory Chichimeca raids, which in turn justified further Spanish slaving incursions (*entradas*). The soldiers sold captive Chichimecas to newly wealthy miners (for a fraction of the price set on the lives of enslaved Africans) to be set to work in their mines and on land they were beginning to claim and convert to ranches and wheat fields.*

On December 15, 1555, the second viceroy of New Spain, Luis de Velasco ordered the creation of a *villa* (town) and a *presidio* (fort) was soon built.

Four years later, on December 17, 1559, the viceroy finally granted the actual title villa and mandated the organization of a town council by January 1, 1560. The village thus became Villa de San Miguel. The document read in part that "in order to avoid the killings and robberies which the Chichimecas have carried out on the road to Zacatecas, let there be founded at the village of San Miguel a Spanish city for the security of that road." The road, of course, was the Camino Real, (the Royal Road), along which the silver from Zacatecas, Guanajuato, and later, San Luis Potosí, was carried to Mexico City, and thence, via Veracruz, to Spain.

After the tiny settlement was granted the status of villa, the town grew rapidly. The lands around San Miguel presented optimal conditions for raising cattle. As the town grew in size, settlements were made along the San Miguel River and its tributaries. Many of the churches, chapels, and shrines remain, evidence of the faith and dedication of the indigenous people.

The viceroy also encouraged San Miguel's growth by sending more Tarascan and Otomí Indians. At the end of his term in office, between 1563 and 1564, Velasco granted more land to the Spaniards who lived in the location. This situation brought forth a greater stability in the area, since the colonists themselves defended their land and property.

In 1560 a Spanish settler, Alonso Moreno Morezón, was granted a gift of "a site and spring to build a batán, a fulling mill, in the understanding that he may not sell it for six years though he may lose it." (A *batán*, a water-driven mill, was used in tanneries and for textile production. Fulling is a step in woolen cloth-

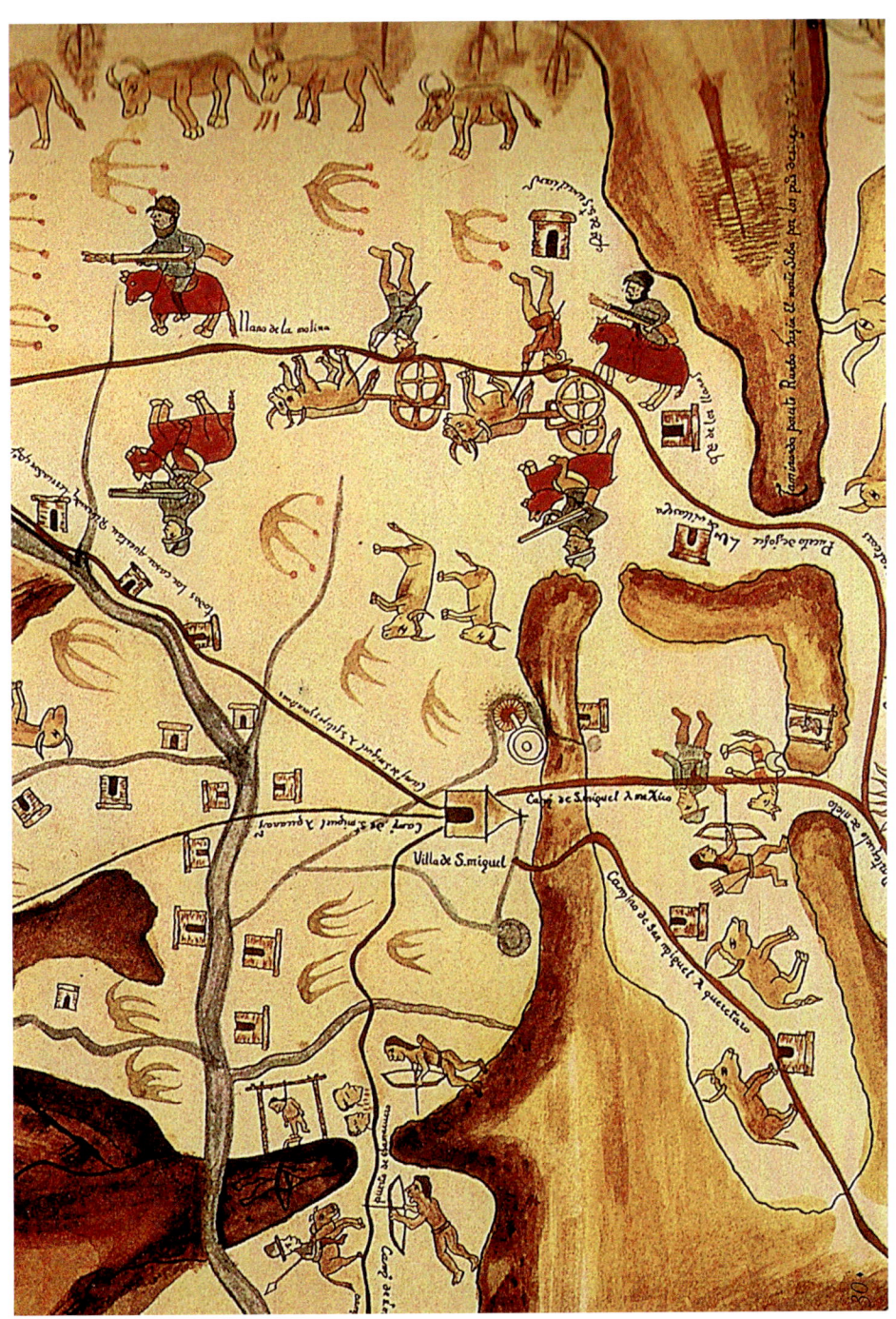

making which involves the cleansing of wool to eliminate oils, dirt, and other impurities.) The mill was built below what is now called El Charco del Ingenio.

Similar gifts were made to others to build mills and other enterprises, always on the condition that the site not be sold or traded for a period of years.

In 1564 a parish was established by order of Vasco de Quiroga, the bishop of Michoacán. Shortly afterward, construction was begun on the first church in San Miguel, San Rafael (the church with the clock tower), for many years after called *Parroquia Vieja* or *Templo de la Fundación*.

Ordered by the King of Spain, the first known map of San Miguel and surrounding areas was produced in 1580. Probably painted by a *tlacuilo* (an indigenous painter-scribe) on paper made of maguey, it shows in remarkable detail sites of the Spanish garrisons, location of churches, areas of economic activity, as well as sources of water, the most important being Ciénega de Landeta (shown near a mill) and El Chorro (shown being used for drinking water and irrigation).

In 1580 the Villa de San Miguel also reported that there were 20 Spanish households, 10 African slaves, and uncounted Otomí. (Nearly a quarter million African slaves came to Mexico, about the same number as Spaniards, mostly males.)

In 1602, taking advantage of the same water source, "a stream and pond to be used for the production of sugar cane" was licensed to Francisco Mexía, thus giving birth to the name *Charco del Ingenio* ("*charco*" means pond and "*ingenio*" refers to a mill or any water-driven machinery).

Between 1546 and 1598 the cycle of deceits, provocations, and reprisals known as the Chichimeca War became a cruel way of life on the northern frontier. Over the same decades the lands of the Chichimecas were quietly invaded by new occupants—not Spaniards but the cattle they had introduced to the Americas, running wild from herds established in central Mexico.

By the 1570s wild cows and horses in the hundreds of thousands roamed the Bajío or flatlands around Guanajuato. Following the cattle came more Spanish ranchers, who were quick to claim them and the lands they grazed on, eager to profit from the sale of their hides and tallow, and outraged by Chichimeca raids on "their" cattle and "their" lands—incursions that they denounced in strident terms.

Three decades after the founding of San Miguel, the fourth viceroy of New Spain, Martín Enríquez de Almanza, begged for help from the King of Spain:

> *A group of Indians the locals call the Chichimeca ... who were to be conquered are up in arms and rebellious against the service of God and His Majesty. ... If all the Spaniards living here were to group together to punish them, they would not constitute a strong enough force, because there is no specific place where they can be located, and their bows and arrows travel like the deer, feeding only on herbs and roots. ... They have thousands of tricks to search for and find the Spaniards until they ambush them along forced passes and roads. They steal and kill with unbelievable cruelty. ... I have done what we could to stop this ... spending much of His Majesty's money ... but it has not been enough. If only His Majesty could make up His mind and order them hunted down with blood and fire. ...*

Punitive expeditions were sent out with Spanish soldiers and their horses, sometimes with more than a thousand Tarascans. But nothing came of these efforts.

The killings and robberies, of course, were not one-sided, and there were complaints from the clergy that evangelization was made more difficult. In a letter to the king in 1561, Bishop Vasco de Quiroga complained:

> *Quite recently, the Chichimeca have been threatened and kept from coming [to Spanish settlements]. ... This will hinder the pious task of baptism, because they [Spaniards] are out hunting these poor creatures. There are certain Spaniards who have built a village called San Miguel with the Viceroy's approval. ... They have Indians and Negroes whom they capture nearby and they turn them into slaves and throw them into the mines or they sell them as they do. The worst thing is that they do the same thing with the women and boys and girls and even babies clinging to the women's breasts, who come here to be baptized. This is totally against that dictated by His Majesty who has stated that no Chichimeca is to be turned into a slave or captured. ...*

For half a century the tribes resisted. What was not achieved by the soldiers was accomplished by the missionaries, especially the Jesuits. By the late 1500s the Chichimecas had been effectively subdued, evangelized, and bought off. The "people of war," as the Spaniards called them, were ultimately defeated  and civilized by the priests. The fighting subsided in the last decade of the 16th century when the viceroy, Luis de Velasco II, with the help of missionary clergy, inaugurated a policy of reconciliation. In return for annual supplies of cattle and clothing, many of the natives were persuaded to put down their weapons. The Chichimeca War lasted until 1598, when a peace accord was reached in the town of San Luis (later renamed "San Luis de la Paz").

The next century was to be relatively peaceful. In a very short time the Villa de San Miguel became one of the most prosperous towns in New Spain and by the end of the 17th century was commonly, although not officially, known as San Miguel el Grande.

In 1619 there were "36 Spanish residents ... 25 Spanish 'young men and women,' 20 slaves, 50 mulattoes and free blacks, some 300 married Indians and another 100 widowers or single."

Over the next 100 years San Miguel became one of the great textile centers in Mexico. Although finer clothes and materials had to be purchased from Spain, *manta* (muslin, a cotton fabric), could be produced in New Spain. And with the importation of sheep, wool products also dominated the textile market.

The introduction of livestock—sheep, goats, horses, and cows—made the leather industry possible. Dozens of tanneries and slaughterhouses operated along the street now called Tenerías, near the Regadera arroyo, and also along Calle Santo Domingo and the Atascadero arroyo. Saddles and other leather products from San Miguel became prized throughout Mexico. Iron products such as stirrups, spurs, branding irons, machetes, swords, and knives were also produced locally.

A never-ending stream of mules and muleteers carrying silver to Mexico City, and returning with needed supplies had to be housed, fed, and supplied. The street called Mesones offered accommodations for the wealthier muleteers and their animals. Although there were a half dozen presidios between Zacatecas and San Miguel, the trek must have been difficult and dangerous. The word "travail" is rooted in "travel" and it was no doubt a relief to reach a mesón in San Miguel at the half-way point between Zacatecas and Mexico City.

By 1640 there were about 600 inhabitants in San Miguel, with several thousand rural dwellers living on or near dozens of haciendas that raised cattle and grew wheat and corn.

In the late 17th and early 18th centuries, the Fertile Crescent between Guanajuato and Querétaro known as the Bajío became an economic powerhouse. Hundreds of haciendas were devoted to raising wheat and livestock, primarily sheep, whose wool fostered a burgeoning local textile industry. (In 1740 the Canal family owned more than 30,000 sheep that grazed in pastures around the town.) In addition, the fabulous wealth created by the silver mines fed a vigorous commerce in cities across the region. San Miguel el Grande, especially, reaped the benefits.

By the middle of the 18th century San Miguel was the leading producer of woolen textiles in the district of Guanajuato, second only to Querétaro in all of New Spain and had become famous for its weaving: sarapes, blankets, and hats. There were also many candle factories using the tallow wax from slaughtered cattle.

Toward the end of the 18th century a government census showed 18 textile looms owned by Spaniards and 348 owned by Indians. After the devastation caused by the War of Independence it would be another 100 years before as many looms were in operation again.

A clerical census of 1754 showed a population of about 25,000, with two-thirds living in the city and counted as Hispanic (Spaniards, mestizos, and mulattoes) and the rest as indigenous. The population of the urban area of San Miguel had increased five times in the previous century, to over 15,000 inhabitants, a number unmatched by any city in British America.

In September of 1764 a Capuchin friar, Francisco de Ajofrín, visited San Miguel and wrote the first description of the town and even managed to draw a

San Miguel El Grande in 1764, by Francisco de Ajofrín (detail)

(Red circles added for clarity)

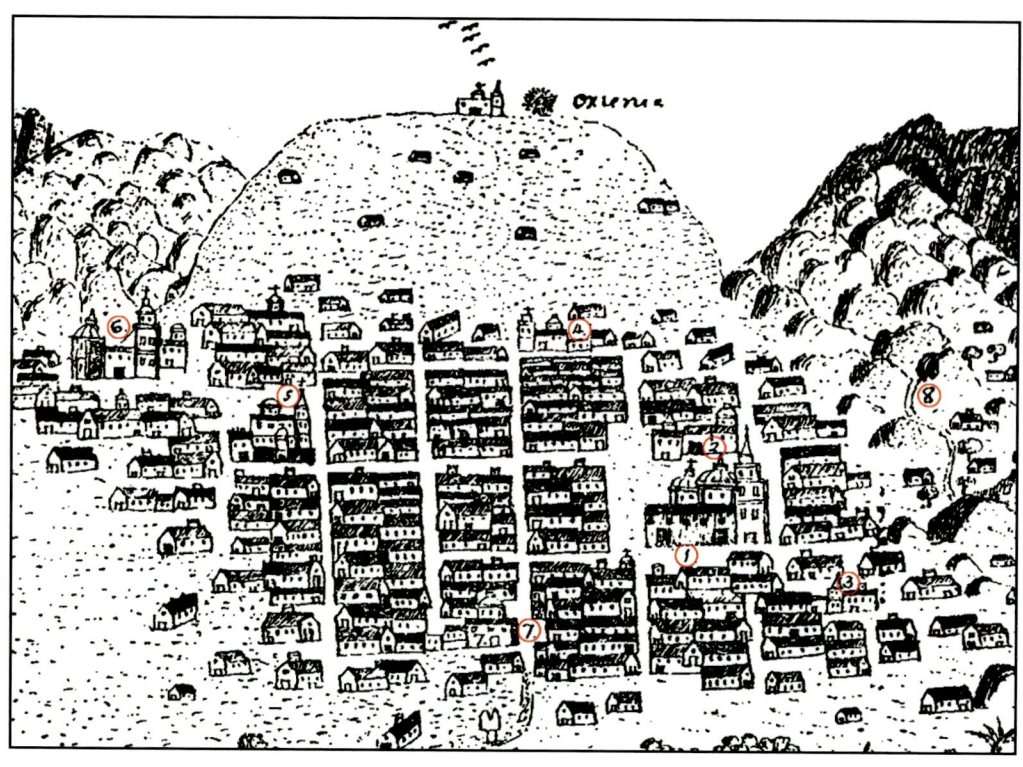

1 *Iglesia Parroquial*	1 Parish Church
2 *Convento que hoy tienen los religiosos de la Concepción*	2 Convent that Conceptionist sisters have today
3 *Beaterio de Franciscanas*	3 Franciscan lay community quarters
4 *Beaterio de Dominicas*	4 Dominican lay community quarters
5 *Convento de Padres Observantes*	5 Observant Fathers' Convent
6 *Oratorio de San Felipe Neri y Colegio*	6 Oratorio of San Felipe Neri and College
7 *Convento que se está fabricando para las Madres de la Concepción*	7 Convent being built for the Conceptionist nuns
8 *Fuente del Chorrillo*	8 El Chorrillo spring

crude map. Early in his commentary he described the difficulty of travel, especially during the rainy season, since there were no bridges:

> *I left towards the Villa of San Miguel el Grande, which is 8 leagues [about 15 miles] away, unable to find shelter until I reached the river [Río Laja] located a league from the villa. I was distraught by fatigue and thirst, by the rocky road and for not being able to find water anywhere. … The river was rough and upon trying to cross it I was dragged by the current and my head grew dizzy, so I gave up and a good man carried me to the other side not without trouble, because of the force of the water. I arrived to the famous villa of San Miguel el Grande in the afternoon of September 12.*

He then commented on the climate, trade, and architecture of the town and the skills of the local artisans:

> *San Miguel is sited on a hillside … and is located between Querétaro, to the south, and Guanajuato, to the west. It features a very healthy climate, with benign winds and sweet waters, in particular the spring they call the Chorillo, which is located in an extremely lush neighborhood. The town has a large population with rich commerce. … Its population has grown, as has its wealthy trade. … [San Miguel] now has a growing population of more than 3000 families of Spaniards, mestizos and mulattoes, and also a large number of Indians who speak Otomí and live in the town's barrios, on its haciendas, and work in its textile factories. There is a convent of the Padres Observantes, with the beautiful chapel of the Tercera Orden; the Oratorio of San Felipe Neri, with a school for younger and older students and also a school for children, all directed by the Fathers of the Oratory; and there is the sumptuous chapel of Our Lady of Loreto, richly adorned by its special benefactor, don Manuel de la Canal. … Currently they are building a magnificent convent called Las Monjas de la Concepción, with a school for children. … In San Miguel el Grande there are also many fruits, in particular, grapefruits, lemons, oranges, etc. In the barrios of the town are big textile factories and workshops where they make exquisite fabrics, almost as fine in quality as those from Segovia. … With needle embroidery, women produce bedspreads or blankets for the beds, and*

> *rugs or carpets for the floors; with great beauty and art. I have seen some works of this kind, with such good taste, like those made in Europe.*

In 1767 another visitor, P.M.F. Pagas, wrote that San Miguel el Grande was "larger and more beautiful than any town he had seen so far in New Spain," and continued, "The inns are large handsome buildings, but … destitute of both furniture and provisions. The houses are good and the places of public resort, such as walks, squares, and gardens, delightful." He called attention to the luxury of the great families, their gambling habits and the grandeur of their houses, the splendor of their furniture, their many domestics, their carriages drawn by four or six mules, "all in contrast to the poor, who dress in rags and are the victims of every vice." He described the Indians as being oppressed and unhappy, and living in a state of utmost squalor.

Ten years later, in 1777, a Spanish friar, Juan Agustín de Morfi, approached San Miguel from the east, "by way of a bad road," and marveled at the countryside:

> *We entered a beautiful plateau lush with mesquite, huisache, and nopal, with good and firm soil; there is a hacienda on either side, with fences made of loose and well placed stone creating a wall at elbow height that goes on until just outside San Miguel el Grande. At this villa, the land turns into a very deep canyon that would be very hard to climb down into had the neighbors not widened the road a bit and badly set it with cobblestones here and there. We had barely come to the end of the hill road and looked over the edge of the canyon when we saw a beautiful object: we were suddenly before an aerial view of the villa at our feet. The Villa of San Miguel el Grande is shaped as an amphitheater at the foot of a cliff and creates a beautiful effect when upon entering it one suddenly discovers it in whole. Its neighborhoods are many and simple with a better society than that of Querétaro; it features a very good parish church with a beautiful and outstanding chamber. Under the chamber, there is a vault destined to serve as a sepulcher for priests. Its construction, soundness and lights are admired by even the most intelligent. The priests' quarters must be worth, some say, between 10 and 12 thousand pesos. The streets, though well traced, are uncomfortable due to the roughness of the ter-*

rain and it is impossible to ride a carriage without the risk of its being overturned. The main plaza features bad paving; one of its sides is occupied by two parish

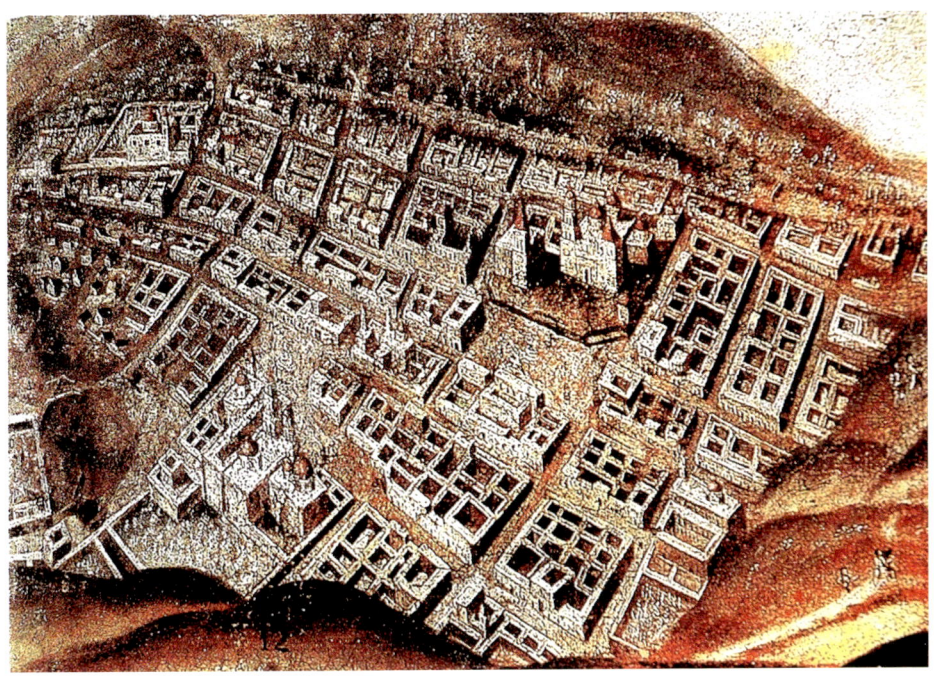

churches, old and new; the other three sides are private homes with no architecture and less magnificence. The rest of the buildings, though some are made of stone and feature a second floor, are mostly low and made from adobe, which makes the place look poor.

It is clear from his description that the great buildings ringing the Jardín had not yet been built.

The year 1777 also saw the publication of the *"Descripción de la Villa de San Miguel el Grande,"* a remarkable survey made at the request of King Charles III of Spain, produced by a priest at the Oratorio who was also a professor at the Colegio de San Francisco de Sales, Dr. Juan Benito Díaz de Gamarra. It described, among other things, the history, geography, and natural history of the area, with lists of the names of plants, herbs, insects, fruits, and even snakes.

The Villa of San Miguel el Grande ... is one of the most beautiful and celebrated in this northern America. ... It is the main town in the jurisdiction and is home to a mayor and town council with congressmen, an attorney, etc. It also features a parish, though its extension is smaller than that of the mayor's jurisdiction. It is founded on two hillsides, one named Moctezuma facing west and another one called San Antonio facing east. The villa faces south. It was founded by Spaniards and Tlascaltecas [sic], who conquered the Chichimeca Indians who inhabited the region, thus the main population includes Spaniards, Mestizos, Mulattoes, and Indians, who live in the 48 abundant cattle-raising haciendas. Some hold jobs as operators and drudges, others rent farmland, and others have jobs in the villa, where they have an Indian governor and officers of the republic. They all speak Otomí.

The water in the villa is healthy, especially that of a natural spring flowing from the high peaks at the foot of the Moctezuma. This spring is commonly called El Chorro, and it supplies almost all the public and private fountains due to its height and speed, which allows it to travel through underground pipes. This water is also used for the numerous orchards in the main ward of Guadiana. There is another spring of fine and clean water, not far from the villa, they call the Sieneguita that feeds the neighborhoods of Santo Domingo, Tecolote, Palmar, and some public and private fountains.

One league from Villa of San Miguel, on the west, is the river they call San Miguel, which elsewhere is called La Laja. During the rainy season, it carries a large amount of water. ... It flows through the new village of Los Dolores, one league [sic] away, through the Sanctuary of Jesus Nazareno of Atotonilco, of which we shall talk later.

There is only one bridge over it, at a hacienda they call La Quemada, 13 leagues north a quarter northwest from there. Mostly, it flows precipitously, and since it carries much water during the rainy season, it is commonplace that several people drown every year. Besides this sad condition, trade with other lands of the inte-

rior and with Guanaxuato, as was seen in 1767, when a commission from San Miguel headed for Guanaxuato could not arrive in time because the river tide was high; the commissioner could not cross the river until three days later, after the business had taken place. Besides this, there is always some delay in the weekly mail during the rainy season.

The climate in this villa is temperate though more prone to cold than heat. ... Abundant rainfall refreshes the air in the months of June, July, and August.

Prevailing wind comes from the east, north and northeast. The latter are very strong and usually last up to 8 days. They are bad for people's heads, because they lose their temperature if they are not well protected, and they usually cause flues, colds, and pneumonias, because they close the skin pores and condense body fluids. On the other hand, they are healthy because they rid the atmosphere of thick or infested vapors, so disease does not last long when the northeast wind blows, because, as we said, the wind is almost continuous.

The northeast wind brings about another damage in that it destroys the clouds during the rainy season, so even though there are good clouds in the area, when this wind blows they disappear, leaving behind a clear sky.

The rainy season begins in the summer, during early May, and finishes in autumn, in late September or early October. Rain is usually very copious. Storms appear when the eastern wind blows. Every year, three or four lightning bolts hit the villa, most of them on the outskirts and mainly on the hills.

At the end of the 18th century San Miguel had adopted so many patron saints (St. John the Baptist, St. Joseph, the Immaculate Conception, the Virgin of Loreto, the Virgin of Guadalupe, and, of course, St. Michael) that the government of New Spain tried to suppress the many celebrations and use the money spent on them for other things, but the people stubbornly defended their feast days. The city council of San Miguel agreed, and arguing that "the Indians be allowed to continue with their religious festivities and celebrations." The government in Mexico City relented: "Religious manifestations ... must not be limited or restricted."

Ever since the foundation of San Miguel, permission was granted to the Indians so they could celebrate the day of their patron saint, San Miguel Arcángel. Participation was forbidden to the Spanish citizens. "The natives," wrote one observer, "guided by their landowners, would close up the main plaza with makeshift fences in order to fight the wild bulls purchased in nearby haciendas. ... Initially amusement for the locals alone, the celebration soon turned into a noisy fair offering comedy, gambling, cockfights, public dances, and other attractions to lure visitors from the remotest places in the region." A formal bullring was eventually built several blocks from the plaza. A budget summary in the 1780s showed that nearly 50 percent of the town's annual revenue came from admissions to the bullring.

ANNUAL REVENUE FROM THE BULLRING	1975 PESOS
REVENUE FROM THE SALE OF CORN	1514 PESOS

Among expenses listed were the following:

FOR REPAIRS TO THE SLAUGHTERHOUSE AND FIXING OF THE CLOCK	26 PESOS
FOR KEEPING THE GARBAGE CART AND FEEDING THE STALLION THAT PULLS IT	70 PESOS
FOR REPAIRS AND CLEANING OF FOUNTAINS AND SEWERS	20 PESOS
TOWN CRIER'S SALARY	40 PESOS

"The Year of Famine" occurred in 1785. After a severe drought and a summer with almost no rainfall, a series of frosts decimated the harvest in much of the Bajío. Thousands of people died. The government attempted to curtail the hoarding of cereals, to no avail. The famine lasted well into 1786.

By the 1790s San Miguel de Allende was one of the most important cities of New Spain with a population of around 12,000 (not counting the Indians), among them 19 owners of haciendas, 12 members of the clergy, and 43 doctors, lawyers, teachers, and other literate professionals. Only 40 *peninsulares*, those born in Spain, lived in town; 30 were merchants, seven were government officials, and three were *hacendados*, landowners or cattle ranchers.

Fearful of a possible invasion by the hated French, the viceroy in 1794 had ordered the creation of a number of regiments to be scattered throughout the country. San Miguel el Grande had to come up with its own regiment. The order was received with great enthusiasm by the citizens and donations of money, horses, and weapons were readily acquired. Narciso de la Canal (see Notables, page 131) promised to provide clothes for 300 men, which, calculated at 80 pesos per person, came to 24,000 pesos. This response was rewarded by the viceroy who allowed the company to be promoted to Dragoon Regiment, and add "of the Queen." The city council, deeply grateful for such an honor, assured the viceroy, "This city council will never have words to express the joy that His Excellency has given us with the designation of the Queen's Regiment of San Miguel el Grande, which shall insure the loyalty that our best wishes shall never surpass." Little did the San Miguel city council suspect that fifteen years after their guarantee of loyalty that same regiment would help bring about independence.

All the regimental posts were taken up by residents of San Miguel. Narciso de la Canal became colonel, Juan María Lanzagorta was appointed lieutenant colonel, Domingo de Allende became first lieutenant, and his brother Ignacio Allende was appointed second lieutenant. The latter was presented to the viceroy by the city council on August 25, 1795, and described as being "twenty-seven years old, single, strong and apt for a military career." Also to be appointed were a sergeant major, three sergeants, two captains, four corporals, a drummer, and twelve soldiers. Juan Aldama was accepted as standard bearer. In the following year the regiment had swollen to 400 fully armed men. For a time the regiment was billeted in Jalapa and San Luis Potosí.

At the start of the 19th century some 20,000 souls lived in San Miguel el Grande. A census report listed that there were 6 neighborhoods, 72 city blocks, 9 churches, 1,214 houses, 23 public fountains, and 200 private ones. In 1802 public baths were built at the Chorro spring, paid for by the Canal family.

In 1808 Ignacio Allende, now a captain, was back in San Miguel el Grande from his tour of duties in Jalapa and San Luis Potosí. Napoleon had invaded Spain and installed his brother on the throne. King Carlos IV had abdicated. Spain was a culturally impoverished backwater, fallen on hard times, with a brutal, decadent ruling class and a fanatical clerical class. Nevertheless, having the hated French rule the country (and its colonies) was intolerable to most of the Creoles (those of pure Spanish blood, but born in America), who had for centuries been treated as second-class citizens.

There were other reasons for discontent. In 1804, one of the measures that shook the inhabitants of New Spain was the Royal Decree of the Consolidation that obligated the Church, which had made loans to farmers, miners, and landowners, to call in the loans and send the monies to Spain. This resulted in the ruin of many and reinforced the big differences between the Criollos and the Mestizos.

The crisis was one of the principal reasons for the War of Independence, along with the drought and famine that in 1809 devastated the region and caused the increase in prices that fueled popular discontent.

In 1809 Allende became involved in a conspiracy to promote independence. (It was famously said that when he was quartered in Jalapa he had written in charcoal on the wall of the barracks, "Independence, you cowardly Creoles"). Secret meetings were held under the guise of dancing or literary parties in the house of Allende's brother, Domingo, on the corner of Reloj and the Plaza Principal. There were also meetings in Querétaro. To avoid suspicion and the opposition of the Church, recruiting a priest was discussed. Allende contacted the parish priest of Dolores, Miguel Hidalgo, who enthusiastically went along with the revolutionaries. It was decided that the rebellion should be launched on September 29, taking advantage of the fiestas and the symbolism of San Miguel Day. But on September 15, when the plot was discovered, Hidalgo and Allende (who was in Dolores) were warned. They decided to start the insurgency at dawn the following day.

September 16, 1810, was a Sunday, market day. Hidalgo rang the parish bell, gathered the Indians at the foot of the steps leading to the church, and proclaimed the famous "*Grito*," The Cry of Independence. The exact words have been lost to history, but they probably included "Long live Mexico, Death to the *Gachupines*, and Long live the Virgin of Guadalupe."

(The reason that the *Grito* is now given on the evening of September 15 is that president Porfirio Díaz, in a typical self-absorbed gesture during the centennial celebrations of the War of Independence in 1910, decided to give the *Grito* late in the evening of September 15: his 80th birthday.)

Perhaps 600 Indians set out on that Sunday morning to begin the liberation of New Spain from the hated *gachupines* (those who wear spurs). The army, according to the historian Enrique Krauze, was "an unruly mob of peasants and Indians, armed with stones, with sticks, with crude lances, without organization of any kind. … Mixed with the half-naked, hungry hordes were countless women dressed in rags. … There were whole families. … It was like the ancient Aztec migrations."

The march toward San Miguel and independence began. They left with Father Hidalgo in the lead, towards the Hacienda de la Erre, about four miles away, where Allende, who had left a little later, caught up with them. The insurgents carried 18 Spanish prisoners, all *peninsulares* living in Dolores. At the hacienda, which was managed by Miguel Malo (one of the rebels), the leaders had lunch. In the afternoon the ragtag army marched toward the Santuario de Atotonilco, 12 miles away in the direction of San Miguel. At the Sanctuary, already much revered in Mexico, Hidalgo took a banner with the image of the Virgin of Guadalupe, which famously became the independence movement's standard. By early evening the "army" had made its way to the center of San Miguel.

Allende's first act was to put the Spaniards they had brought from Dolores into safekeeping, so he headed for the Colegio de San Francisco de Sales, empty at the time because the students were on vacation. He left them in the custody of Juan Aldama. Then he and Hidalgo went to negotiate the surrender of the Spaniards of San Miguel, who were gathered upstairs in the Casas Reales, the City Hall. They were also taken to the Colegio.

A mob had gathered on the corner of San Francisco and Reloj, at a store called La Princesa and began looting. Within minutes the store was totally plundered. Sword in hand, Allende dispersed the crowd, but not before another nearby store was ransacked also. The houses of the Spaniards, though, were not threatened. The following morning brought a few more looting attempts, but the crowd was again assuaged. At four in the afternoon a meeting was held and a new City Council appointed, with Ignacio Aldama as mayor. On September 18 organizing of the insurgent army began with a cadre of about 200 officers and soldiers from the Dolores and San Miguel regiments. The Indians and townspeople, now numbering around 5,000, were provided with spears, knives, machetes, slingshots, and sticks.

Early in the morning of September 19, the insurgents began their move toward Celaya. The Spanish prisoners, on foot and tied up, were also marched amid the fully armed regiments. Celaya was looted and the army continued toward Guanajuato, where on September 28 the insurgents, now numbering about 20,000, surrounded the *Alhóndiga de las Granaditas*, a huge grain storage building, where the Spanish citizens of Guanajuato had fortified themselves. A miner nicknamed "*Pípila*" (see Notables, page 136) distinguished himself by burning down one of the granary's doors, thus allowing the mob to enter the building, where a massacre took place.

With perhaps 75,000 men the forces continued toward Mexico City, but unaccountably Hidalgo decided not to pursue this course, and the army turned northward. For the next several years the independence movement floundered. Hidalgo, Allende, the Aldama brothers, and other rebels were caught by royalist forces and executed. It would be another ten years before Independence was achieved.

San Miguel el Grande was recaptured a month later by General Manuel Flon, Conde de la Cadena, who was the commander of one of several armies the viceroy had directed to destroy the rebels. Flon had sworn to destroy the town, the place where the rebellion had started. Many of the residents left or took refuge in churches and convents, locked up their stores and houses. On October 25 the Count entered a virtually abandoned city. He did not destroy it, as he had vowed, but encouraged his troops to loot the houses of de la Canal, Allende, Aldama, Malo, and many others. Three days later, Flon left San Miguel for Celaya, "leaving nothing behind. There were no jewels or valuable furniture that he did not take," wrote de la Canal in a statement. (After the War of Independence was over, many of the families were reimbursed by the Mexican government.)

Only about 5,000 people remained in the once prosperous city. Peasants and factory workers had joined the insurgent army. The regiment was engaged in battles in faraway places, its leaders killed. With industry paralyzed, commerce barely existed. For the first time in its history, poverty struck. Since the town had been rich and famous for so long that for more than a decade, until the war ended in 1821, San Miguel was the target of the greed and ambition of both sides in the conflict. There were countless "confiscations," lootings, and attacks, both by insurgents and royalists. Claiming to be fighting against the Spanish government, bandits terrorized much of the country, especially in the Bajío. They threatened and looted San Miguel a number of times, sometimes with as many as 2,000 men.

Independence was gained in 1821. It is thought that 600,000 lives were lost during the struggle. The looms and tanneries in San Miguel, which had stopped their production due to the lack of raw materials, eventually restarted operations. Although nearby rural communities prospered from agriculture, the town stagnated—ironically preserving the architectural monuments of the 18th century for lack of funds. San Miguel had become a place of little commerce and little industry, no longer "el Grande." Mexico began to enjoy a certain peace. Although political struggles continued, robberies and violence subsided, communications were restored and roads eventually became safe again. San Miguel's old splendor, however, had vanished. Industry and trade returned, but its effects were smaller. The construction fever of the 18th century did not continue into the 19th century so that much of the inner city today looks much like it did in colonial times.

On March 8, 1826, via a decree from the Congress of Guanajuato, San Miguel el Grande was renamed San Miguel de Allende, thus linking the city with its hero. The town of Dolores was renamed Dolores Hidalgo.

In September, 1864, Maximilian von Hapsburg, then the Emperor of Mexico, embarked on a tour of some of the major cities in his new empire. After visiting Morelia, Querétaro, and some smaller towns, he traveled to San Miguel de Allende. After "having to get off the carriage several times because of the bad condition of the roads," he arrived in town in early afternoon on September 14 to be met by a group of the most prominent citizens. Bells tolled, and many of the houses were decorated with flags and flowers. After a Mass in the Parroquia and a quick visit to the crypt underneath the church (which he pronounced "Fit for a king"), he was entertained, visited the jail, the school, and the hospital. In a hurry to reach Dolores Hidalgo to give the annual Grito, the cry for Mexican independence, he left San Miguel on September 15. He had been in town less than 20 hours, never to return. In June, 1867, as the forces of Benito Juárez gained control of the country, Maximilian was arrested in Querétaro, court-martialed and executed by a firing squad. The Empress Carlota, who had returned to Europe in 1866 to seek support for her husband, became insane and was admitted to an asylum in Belgium, where she lived until 1927, never regaining her sanity.

The 1900 census showed there were more than 40,000 people living in the municipio, but with fewer than 10,000 people in the city itself. The first years of the century saw the opening of the cotton textile and thread factory La Aurora. Almost a thousand workers found employment. The Mexiquito neighborhood was created to accommodate many of the workers of the factory with homes.

In 1903 a mule-drawn tram service was introduced between Calle San Francisco and the newly built railroad station, 1.5 miles west of town. The tram ran on wooden rails.

In 1906 the Las Colonias dam was constructed at the Charco del Ingenio and the great iron tube that conveyed the water from the reservoir to the generators at the La Aurora factory was connected.

In 1908 during the Ignacio Hernández Macías administration, electricity was introduced in many of the streets in the Centro of San Miguel.

A traveler in the same year, Adolfo Dollero, began his description of the city thus:

San Miguel de Allende is not ugly. It has a population of around 10 thousand people, but was bigger in the past, when the Zacatecas hacienda owners sent their sheep here to be sheared. The locals made multicolored serapes from the wool. Serapes are still made today, as are shawls of unquestionable fame; however, many workers have migrated in search of higher wages and the wool industry has decreased in importance ...

There is plenty of water; part of it comes from the Laja River and is used as irrigation, and part comes from the numerous springs. A stream of crystal-clear water always runs down the streets of San Miguel and, once it goes through the city, irrigates fertile orchards located farther down the hill.

The city features a few buildings of sound construction, from the times of the Spanish domination, and a pretty Gothic-style cathedral [sic]. It is provided with potable water and electric streetlights. The garden in the plaza is usually crowded during concert nights and the people are courteous and well mannered. ... We visited several picturesque places in the vicinity, including the Aurora textile factory, small, but splendidly equipped with state-of-the-art English machinery. ... This factory was powered by hydraulic energy provided by a large reservoir and a spring that belongs to the factory.

Two years later, the Revolution began. Although never the scene of serious fighting, San Miguel nevertheless experienced several incidents.

On May 18, 1911, a riot ensued when hundreds tried to burn down City Hall, resulting in the destruction of part of the archives. The building was repaired and rebuilt two years later.

In 1921 a small art school, called "La Princesa," was opened in the building on the corner of Reloj (then still spelled "Relox") and San Francisco. Sculpting and music were taught. It was a short-lived enterprise and it would be several decades before San Miguel again had an art school.

In 1924, shortly before the outbreak of the three-year Church vs. State conflict that came to be known as the Cristero War, a rebellion against the federal government took place in the rural community of Tambula de Guadalupe, about six miles from San Miguel. About 30 people, shouting "Long Live Christ the King," took up arms against government troops. All were killed.

In 1930 the Guanajuato Chamber of Commerce published a directory extolling the many advantages of investing in the state. The booklet provides some information on San Miguel's commercial scene. In addition to traditional economic activities such as the production of cotton shawls and woolen serapes, the manufacture of iron and tin products, and tanning of leather hides, there were six grain merchants in town and several cereal storage buildings. Although this clearly was not a complete list, the directory mentioned that in San Miguel there were ten grocery stores, eight clothing stores, six notions and hardware stores, three drugstores, one shoe store, one bank, one hotel, a soap factory, and a textile factory. Three lawyers and one engineer had offices in town. No mention was made of doctors. Fourteen trucks and six automobiles were registered. (The few roads were so bad that during the rainy season travel to nearby Celaya was only possible by train.)

The population of the municipio (and the town) continued to decrease. According to the 1930 census the total population of the municipio was 32,680 with only 8,716 residing in the city of San Miguel. The census also listed 24 rural estates and 232 rural communities (*ranchos*). (In 2009 there were more than 500 ranchos in the county of San Miguel.) Only two percent of the county's 100,000 arable acres was being irrigated. Corn and beans were the important crops, but wheat, alfalfa, chiles, and barley were also cultivated. Maguey succulents were grown for the production of fermented drinks. The census also mentioned that there were 14,000 fruit trees in orchards around the city. More than 60,000 head of cattle, sheep, goats, pigs, horses, and mules had been counted in the municipio.

During the early 1930s, the baths at the waterworks of El Chorro were refurbished and warm water for showers made available.

The mid-1930s saw San Miguel also beginning to be affected by the Great Depression. Exports were curtailed. San Miguel was becoming a ghost town, with many of its houses in ruin. The population was down to about 7,000. But that was about to change. In 1937 two foreigners, one from Peru and one from the U.S., would start the renaissance of San Miguel.

On February 7, 1937, an American artist and writer, Stirling Dickinson (see Notables, page 132) arrived at the train station in San Miguel. On the advice of actor

and singer José Mojica (see Notables, page 137), Dickinson and his Princeton classmate, Heath Bowman, settled in San Miguel to finish work on a novel they were writing. They bought an old tannery on Calle Santo Domingo for 90 dollars.

In that same year another expatriate, this one Chilean, Felipe Cossío del Pomar (see Notables, page 129) arrived in San Miguel. Together with Dickinson, they would forever change the face of San Miguel.

It was not Cossío's first visit to San Miguel. This wealthy Peruvian artist, art critic, and political activist had first seen San Miguel more than a decade earlier. In the fall of 1926, Cossío was exiled from Peru and traveled to Mexico. He also arrived by train in San Miguel. It was not an auspicious first visit. He wrote in his memoir:

> *There had just been a downpour. Crystal clear water was dripping from the long eucalyptus leaves and the train station glistened with moisture. Although the sky provided a beautiful backdrop for the blue mountains in the distance and the stately maguey plants formed elegant frames for the fields, the place couldn't have been called beautiful. The cart rails [leading from the train station to town], the hills colored a dusky red, the shabby grain silos and the little stores, the vendors along the road—all gave the landscape a depressing gracelessness.*
>
> *In the distance we could see the town anchored solidly to sepia-colored hills, creating an enormous stone retablo of rusty red ochres mixed with green splotches of foliage. Under the late afternoon sun, the tile-covered cupolas reflected the jewel-like colors of sapphire, emeralds, topaz. Ever since that moment I have contended that the light in San Miguel de Allende is, above all, iridescent.*
>
> *We traveled the three kilometers into town in a small cart pulled by mules long accustomed to the daily transport of cargo and passengers. The little cart traveled back and forth from train station to town on rickety rails mounted on higher ground to avoid the potholes in the road.*

As we were pulled along in the little cart we were jostled by the mules' persistent efforts as they splashed through the mud. We skirted around stubbled orchards and fields bounded by crumbling walls, every now and then holding back to let groups of work-weary burros pass by. ... Ancient bells tolled. Everything was of bygone times: crumbling stucco buildings, moss-covered plazas, the grass growing between the sidewalks' worn flagstones, the cobblestone streets, the slow amble of the people.

There was only one hotel in town, "one with more flowers and plants than comfort," and there were no restaurants. He stayed for only a short time and was eventually able to return to Peru. It would be nearly a dozen years before he returned to San Miguel de Allende.

In 1937 Cossío de Polmar was once again exiled from Peru and returned to Mexico. In the years to come he would buy a number of properties in San Miguel, beginning with La Ermita, where he entertained famous writers, poets, and musicians. He had paid 200 dollars for this abandoned stage-coach property on the Salida a Querétaro (it was sold in the 1970s to the Mexican movie star and comedian, Cantinflas, who demolished all but the entrance gate and turned it into a condominium hotel). Shortly afterward, Cossío bought the Atascadero ranch (now the Atascadero Hotel) above the city, constructed a road (now the Prolongación Santo Domingo) and built arches at the entrances to the property. The two arches were modeled after a 17th century arch in his hometown of Cuzco, in Peru. He threw himself into the artistic life of the town. He wasn't the only artist, though. A few years earlier the singer and actor José Mojica and the bullfighter Pepe Ortiz (who was also an artist) had built or restored homes in San Miguel and formed a group they called the Society of Friends of San Miguel, whose first projects were repairing street lights, replacing paving stones in the sidewalks and restoring the park. Other well-known Mexican artists joined in the effort: Tata Nacho and Mario Talavero, well-known musicians, the famous singer and native son Pedro Vargas, Miguel Prado, and others. The preservation of San Miguel seemed in good hands. But Cossío del Pomar wanted more than preservation and restoration. He wanted to open an art school.

In the summer of 1937 he began an effort to open a school for artists. The ex-convent of La Concepción, locally known as "Las Monjas," was suggested as a venue. It was almost in ruins. A cavalry regiment had been quartered in the building for years. "No single door was left," reported Cossío, "many of them having been pulled out together with their frames, leaving door jambs of exquisitely carved stone." But because the building was owned by the government and used by the army, federal permission had to be obtained. With the help of friends, including José Vasconcelos, a former Minister of Education, Cossío managed to meet with the president of Mexico, Lázaro Cárdenas, and convinced him of the merits of his proposal. Cárdenas approved of the idea to establish a school in San Miguel de Allende. "The president," Cossío recalled later, "understood fully what I was proposing: to convert a dying town into a university city." The cavalry regiment was given two weeks to evacuate the building. Cossío, a wealthy man, met questions about the economic aspects by insisting he could resolve those without government help. "I have some resources with which I can underwrite the initial installation expenditures. The rest will depend on the reception it has in the foreign community. … We'll sell culture; for the moment that's all the store that I plan to open in San Miguel de Allende will sell."

Stirling Dickinson, who had been involved with Cossío's project from the beginning, became the Associate Director and produced the first catalog, with bios of the faculty the school hoped to entice to teach. Among them were Diego Rivera, José Chavez Morado, Pablo O'Higgins, Federico Cantú, Carlos Mérida—some of the most distinguished painters in Mexico. Five thousand catalogs in English and five thousand in Spanish were sent to colleges and universities throughout the Americas. In 1938 the Escuela Universitaria de Bellas Artes was opened for business.

When the first twelve students arrived in the summer of 1938 before the building was quite ready to receive them they were temporarily housed in the former Colegio Francisco de Sales on the Plaza Cívica. Finding lodging was not difficult, but a lack of bathrooms provided obstacles, with outhouses being the only sanitary facilities. There still wasn't a single restaurant in town, but stalls in the market offered food.

In 1939 the new art school was finally settled in Las Monjas, ready to receive more than 100 students. There were apartments for professors. There were studios, classrooms, and bathrooms with showers, a modern kitchen and a roomy dining hall. The patio had been replanted. Some of the students were housed in the Posada de San Francisco, a new hotel on a corner of the Jardín. Its 15 rooms could accommodate 30 students. Cossío recounted his surprise at the commercial boom his school created: "For each new student there were two merchants. The businessmen of San Miguel de Allende converted their large and stately entrance ways into shops and the windows of their homes into display windows. … The cantinas prospered."

The Escuela Universitaria de Bellas Artes began its third year in 1940. But the war in Europe was beginning to affect the school's enrollment, and when at the end of the following year the attack on Pearl Harbor occurred, Cossío described the changes as "unexpected and huge … my dreams of seeing the school prosper were crumbling." But he kept the school open. Dickinson returned to the U.S., joined the U.S. Army and spent the war years as an interpreter.

The 1940s saw the installation of water and sewage systems in the city. No paved roads yet connected San Miguel with nearby cities; the roads to Querétaro and Guanajuato were described on maps as "all-weather roads," the road to Celaya as "provisional."

In 1942 San Miguel celebrated the fourth centenary of its founding. A statue of the town's founder, Fray Juan de San Miguel, was commissioned and installed in the northwest corner of the Parroquia's atrium. The bullring was renovated and many other buildings spruced up. Still, Cossío del Pomar had written: "The town was losing its traditional flavor. Its tranquility was being disturbed by frugal visitors rapidly passing through. There were countless stores to serve them, yet there was not one book store. San Miguel was losing its way and becoming separated from its noble destiny. …"

At the end of World War II the U.S. Congress approved legislation to help returning veterans adapt to civilian life. The G.I Bill, as it became known, made free university education possible, including study abroad. The Escuela Universitaria de Bellas Artes met the requirements. A stipend of $50 per course per month was allowed for each student.

In 1945 the political situation in Peru had changed again so that Cossío was able to return to his home country. The school had been closed for a short time but Cossío del Pomar found an investor, Alfredo Campanella, who bought his Atascadero property and reopened the school. After his discharge from the Army, Dickinson returned to San Miguel and resumed the position of Associate Director. In 1946 a dozen American students enrolled in the Escuela Universitária. The following year more than 50 attended classes. Several teachers, from the U.S. and Canada, also settled in San Miguel.

Two who were to be among the most famous of the teachers were Leonard and Reva Brooks. Leonard, born in England in 1911, emigrated to Canada at an early age, met and married Canadian-born Reva Brooks, two years younger, in 1935. The artists, she a photographer-to-be and he a painter, arrived in San Miguel in July 1947 after Leonard had received a Canadian government grant to study art in Mexico. He had taught art in a high school in Toronto and when the Escuela Universitaria de Bellas Artes opened again he was recruited by Stirling Dickinson to teach. Reva took up photography shortly after her arrival in San Miguel and within a few years had become an important photographer. The couple helped establish San Miguel de Allende as a world-famous art colony. Reva was named one of the world's top women photographers by the San Francisco Museum of Art. One of her photographs was selected for the famous "Family of Man" exhibition at New York's Museum of Modern Art in 1955. Leonard, who was also a gifted musician (he played first violin with the Guanajuato Symphony for years), published many books about painting and has been exhibited world-wide. Their work is held in collections throughout the world. Reva died in 2004 at age 91.

By 1947 San Miguel de Allende had ten telephones. About 30,000 people lived in the municipio, still only 10,000 in the town itself. Five cars were registered.

There was one taxi. But room and board for students was only $45 a month while the stipend for the returned U.S. veterans for living expenses was $65 a month.

On January 5, 1948, *Life* magazine carried a steamy article about San Miguel and the lifestyle of the veterans, and it caused a small sensation. The headline read: "GI Paradise. Veterans go to Mexico to study art, live cheaply and have a good time." The piece featured photographs of a painting class (small) and a nude model (large-actually the wife of one of the students). Readers were led to believe that GIs were living it up in luxury on their government grants, not mentioning that the majority were serious students. The article read like an advertisement: "The veterans and their wives have come to study painting, ceramics, murals, sculpture, and languages. They find it very pleasant in the quiet little town of San Miguel de Allende, up in the mountains north of Mexico City. The air is crisp, the flowers are bright, the sun is warm, apartments are $10 a month, servants are $8 a month, good rum or brandy 65 cents a quart, cigarettes are 10 cents a package." Not surprisingly, thousands of veterans wrote to the school to register. Lodging for so many people would have been impossible, and Dickinson allowed only about a hundred to attend.

In 1948 Cossío was once again deported from Peru and returned to Mexico. In the meantime, Campanella had hired famous artist David Alfaro Siqueiros as a professor. For a short time Siqueiros taught (and began work on a mural in the ex-convent's dining room). When it became known that Siqueiros was a member of Mexico's Communist Party, the House Un-American Activities Committee in July 1949 bullied the U.S. Embassy to suspend payments and transfer the G.I. students to an art school that had just opened in Morelia. The school was forced to close. Serious disagreements with Campanella over money and other matters (including an alleged physical assault) led to Siqueiros's leaving. Campanella went public with the disagreement, denouncing the painter in full-page ads in Mexico City newspapers. Many famous artists, including Diego Rivera, Frida Kahlo, and Rufino Tamayo came to Siqueiros's aid. After a while, the matter appeared to have been resolved.

At the end of 1949 Cossío made a second attempt to establish a fine arts school in San Miguel. He considered that no building was better suited than the run-down former property of the Canal family on the Ancha de San Antonio, then surrounded by fruit orchards. With his partners, Enrique Fernández Martínez, a former governor of Guanajuato, and American-born wife, Nell Harris, Cossío was able to buy the huge property and restore the buildings. They decided to call it the Instituto Allende. The following year the school opened, affiliated with the University of Guanajuato. Dickinson became director of the arts division.

But on August 12, 1950, unannounced, three agents from Mexico's Department of the Interior arrived in San Miguel with orders to deport the foreign professors. They put Dickinson and eight of his instructors (and their wives) on the train to Laredo. The deportation had apparently been choreographed by Campanella. It was his revenge against Dickinson and Siqueiros and the other instructors. But Dickinson had acquired powerful and influential friends in Mexico, and 12 days later all but Dickinson were allowed to return to San Miguel with their immigration papers in order. With the help of Fernández Martínez, Dickinson was also eventually able to return.

Affiliated with the University of Guanajuato, and accredited by the G.I. Bill administrators, the Instituto began offering academic credit to returning U.S. World War II veterans studying under the American G.I. Bill. Many who came to study were charmed by the culture, the life style, the laid-back atmosphere, and the low cost of living, and they stayed. In the mid-1950s there were probably no more than about 75  foreigners living full-time in San Miguel, along with the same number of students. But an article in the popular magazine *Coronet* began to change that. After noting the low costs for housing and help, the article added: "In San Miguel, though, you are surrounded by stimulating students, artists and writers. Most are young Americans and Canadians, and the fact that you are in the midst of a thriving English-speaking colony eliminates any possibility of loneliness caused by a language barrier." The author included Stirling Dickinson's name and address, and to his chagrin Dickinson received more than 4,000 letters. He sent out a form letter informing his correspondents that there were certain problems in paradise: foreigners couldn't work, nor—at the time—own a house. But many came, although it is not known exactly how many. The great wave of foreign arrivals did not occur until the 1970s.

Seven years after the Instituto was founded, charges against Dickinson surfaced in the U.S. Articles in both *Time* and the *New York Herald Tribune* identified Dickinson as a "mystery man" who played host to Communist meetings in his home in San Miguel. The September 9, 1957, issue of *Time* featured a story, headlined "Red Haven." Part of it read: "But still in Mexico is a thriving colony of wealthy expatriates representing every shade in the Communist spectrum, from parlor pink to Moscow Red. A gathering place for the colony reportedly is the spacious home of Sterling [*sic*] Dickinson, U.S.-born director of art-conscious San Miguel de Allende's biggest art school. A resident of Mexico for 20-odd years, he keeps open house for Communists and fellow travelers." Dickinson's family, which ran one of the most powerful law firms in Chicago, threatened a libel suit. Both publications eventually offered apologies and the House Internal Security Subcommittee publicly admitted that it had leaked erroneous information about Dickinson.

In 1957 a rash of robberies of religious art occurred in San Miguel. Treasures were stolen from the Parroquia, and from the churches of San Rafael, San Francisco, La Tercera Orden, and the Oratorio.

> *The Rancho Atascadero was housing a number of students from the Instituto Allende. There were now three hotels in town but most students lived with Mexican families or rented rooms. The few telephones in town still had only two-digit numbers and most expatriates communicated with their friends and acquaintances using messengers who delivered invitations and information to the recipient's mailbox.*

The population in San Miguel, according to the 1960 census, reached 12,000.

San Miguel was also being discovered as a movie location. The 1960s saw a boom in the making of movies by Mexican companies on location in San Miguel:

"*El Padrecito*" with Cantinflas, "*Toros Bravos*," "*El Caballo de mi General*," "*Serenata*," and several others.

In 1962 the Mexican government opened the Centro Cultural Ignacio Ramírez "El Nigromante" (Bellas Artes) in the ex-convent of La Concepción. For the next 30 years it was to be run by Carmen Masip de Hawkins, another of the principal organizers of the cultural renaissance of San Miguel. She fought for 50 years to preserve the city's architectural heritage. Born in Spain in 1929, she arrived in Mexico (along with nearly a quarter million Spaniards as exiles from the Spanish Civil War) in 1939. She was one the founders of the Biblioteca Pública and the Academia Hispano Americana, a language school. She helped save from demolition the Ángela Peralta Theater, which she then managed for ten years. She headed the Chamber Music Festival for decades. She died in 2004. A *plazuela* on the corner of Mesones and Hernández Macías was named after her, and a bust, sculpted by her husband, was installed next to the entrance to Bellas Artes.

By the early 1970s the population of the city of San Miguel had grown to 15,000 (the ex-pat population hovered around less than 1,000). The road to Querétaro was still a single-lane affair.

Although the population of Mexico in 1945 was only around 20 million people, by 2009 the number had quintupled to nearly 110 million. In the same period the population of the urban area of San Miguel grew from about 9,000 to 70,000 inhabitants. In 1990 there were about 2,500 expats living in San Miguel. The numbers doubled in the next two decades.

At the beginning of the 21st century San Miguel experienced its greatest real estate expansion both in the Mexican and the expatriate communities. Prices soared, especially for houses in or near the historic district. Outlying areas, many along the road north toward Dolores, saw the construction of numerous gated communities, while many new neighborhoods were added around the eastern, western, and southern rim of the city.

Many of the city's churches were rehabilitated. Street surfaces and sidewalks were improved. Hotels proliferated, as did restaurants and shops. Signage for streets and traffic directions were increased. Traffic multiplied and parking became difficult. Several attempts were made to put the electrical, telephone, and

TV cable wires underground, but by the beginning of the 2010 celebrations not one street was totally cleared of wires. Cell phone and other antenna towers proliferated. There were more than 500 communities in the *municipio* and the urban area of San Miguel counted nearly a hundred neighborhoods. Many of the town's government offices had been relocated to the edge of town.

Four and a half centuries after officially being named "Villa de San Miguel," in July 2008, San Miguel de Allende and the nearby Santuario de Atotonilco were officially designated a combined UNESCO World Heritage Site.

Although written many years ago, the words of the novelist Robert Somerlott (who lived in San Miguel for decades) still resonate when he warned against "the whirlwind explorer who deluded himself that the town and its centuries would yield themselves up in a series of glances and snapshots." He noted that "San Miguel is deeper, more varied and complex than even some of its intricate monuments. The best rewards come gradually, unexpectedly, often by accident: the subtle changes of the stones of La Parroquia as the light shifts … and the faces of San Miguel: smiling, weathered, gaunt, enigmatic, mischievous—an endless gallery of portraits."

The Historic District

In July of 1939 the State of Guanajuato made the first attempt to protect the historic heritage of San Miguel. It promulgated a law, "*Ley de Protección de la Ciudad Típica de San Miguel de Allende*." It was a lengthy and serious document that covered every aspect of the city's heritage and history. Unfortunately, not a single section was ever enforced.

More than 40 years later, in 1982, the federal government created a *Zona de Monumentos Históricos* (Historic Monuments Zone) in San Miguel. Three other historic cities in the state were also listed: Mineral de Pozos, Dolores Hidalgo, and Guanajuato (the state capital). This law had more teeth in it and was enforced by INAH, the Instituto Nacional de Antropología e Historia.

The boundaries of the Zone are irregular and follow a meandering course. The northern boundary begins at the corner of Calles Quebrada and Insurgentes, follows a straight line east to the Plaza Cívica, then angles slightly and follows the northern edge of the Plaza to Calle Colegio where it turns north to Puente Umarán on which it turns right, makes a short jog left on Núñez to Calle Homobono, turns right and continues to Calle Aparicio.

The eastern segment follows Aparicio (to the right from Homobono) until almost the end of the Aparicio curve where it turns left into San Dimas, right onto Calvario, left onto Salida a Querétaro, right again on Bajada de la Garita and left again on Calle Barranca until it reaches Calle Huertas.

The southern border begins at this point, following Huertas to Calle Recreo where it makes a small jog right and then left on Calle Terraplén and continues to its end, makes a very small jog to the left on Calle Jesús, turns right onto Tenerías and continues to its end at Zacateros.

The western boundary begins at Tenerías and Zacateros, following the latter to the right on block, left on Calle Pila Seca until it reaches Quebrada, turns right and continues to its intersection with Insurgentes, completing the boundaries and enclosing, according to the official document a total of 68 blocks, a seemingly large area. In fact, the Zone occupies little more than 100 acres (less than one square kilometer) and contains only 34 blocks.

Conspicuous by their exclusion are delightful and pretty streets and alleys like Piedras Chinas, Ánimas, Montes de Oca, the streets around Parque Juárez, and the alleys near the San Juan de Dios neighborhood. The word "gerrymander" does come to mind.

The legislation of the Historic Monuments Zone Act forbids changes to the exteriors of buildings, defines signage and mentions other restrictions. Since the legal border of the Zone runs precisely down the middle of all the streets in question, it can be jarring to see how one side of a street is pristine, while the other side escapes the legal constraints of the Act. Electrical, telephone and cable TV wires were supposed to be buried in 1998, a process that seemed interminable at that time but a dozen years later not a single street is totally devoid of wires.

In 2008 the City of San Miguel de Allende (along with the Santuario de Atotonilco) received the prized **UNESCO** World Heritage Site designation. More than 250 buildings were catalogued in the **UNESCO** zone, with 50 belonging to federal, state, and local authorities and the rest privately held. Although there are no enforcement regulations, UNESCO's Primary Zone is more inclusive than the Historic Monuments Zone.

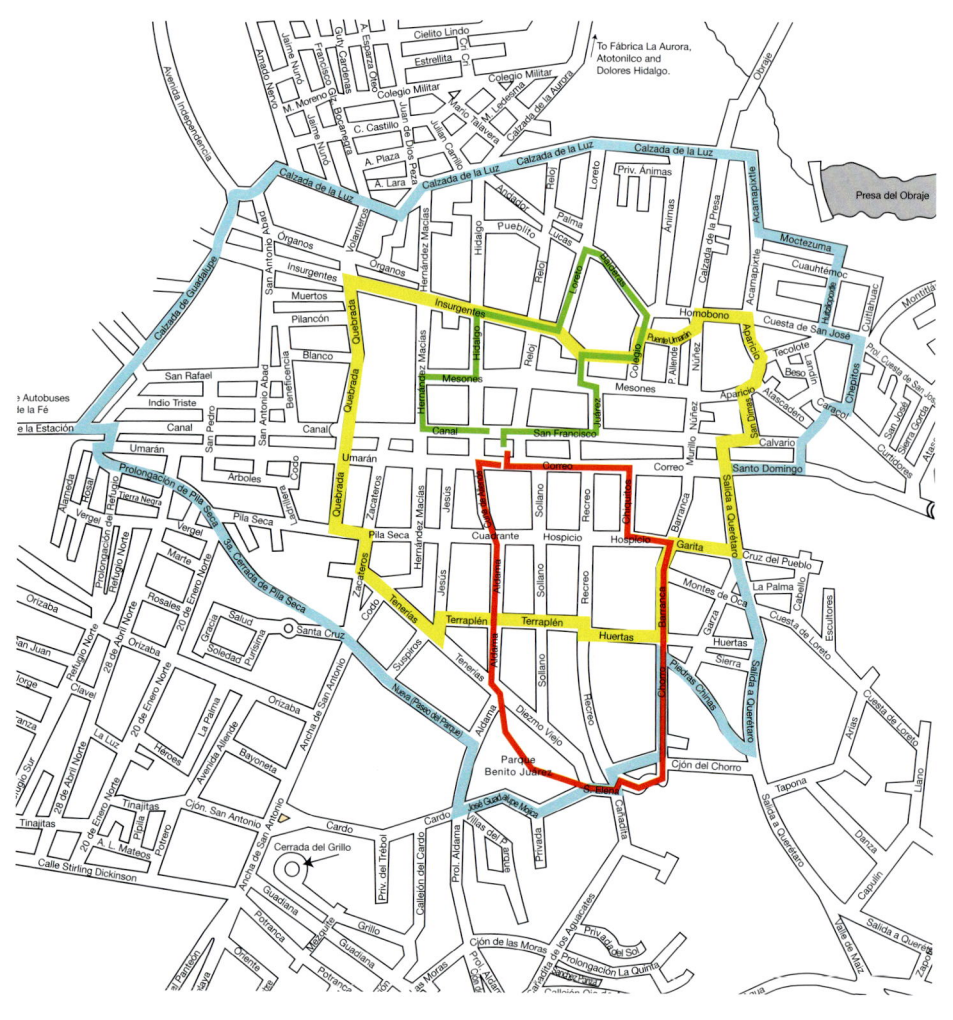

- UNESCO World Heritage Site Boundary
- Historic Center
- Walk 1
- Walk 2

Two Short Walks around Town

Any walking tour of San Miguel naturally begins and ends in the Jardín. "In all of Mexico, you will not find a more beautiful plaza," wrote Norman Ford in his "Fabulous Mexico" in 1970.

These two circular tours, on mostly flat terrain, will allow a leisurely stroll to see many of the most interesting sites and scenes of San Miguel. Both walks can easily be accomplished in a few hours. So, we'll start from the Jardín:

Plaza Principal, the Jardín: Every Mexican town of any size has a plaza, a public square, surrounded by the most important buildings: the church, the city hall, houses of the most prominent citizens, and in earlier times the jail and perhaps a grain storage building. In most cities and towns the main plaza, the *plaza principal*, is called the *zócalo* ("base" in Náhuatl). San Miguel's main plaza officially has several names: *Plaza Principal* or *Plaza Allende*, each name appearing on a sign at a different corner of the plaza. No matter: it is always called the *Jardín*. It wasn't always the Garden. Until 1737 it wasn't even the Plaza Principal. From the mid-1550s until the late 1880s it remained a dusty parade-ground, used as a market space on Sundays.

The urban design of San Miguel was essentially dictated by terrain. The Hill of Montezuma on which the town was built is not a smooth, continuous slope. It was forested, with occasional higher outcroppings and thus it seemed reasonable to site the church on a relatively high spot (closer to God) and to situate the civic buildings on a large, flat area (easier for the people). It worked for almost 200 years: the parish church sat on a slight knoll and the political and commercial center was located on the Plaza de la Soledad, now the Plaza Cívica, which we'll visit on our second walk.

After the first parish church ("*parroquia*") was built in the mid-1580s, the plaza was for a time called *Plaza Parroquial*. In the latter part of the 18th century a fountain was added in the middle, the water piped from the Chorro spring. During the dictatorship of Porfirio Díaz (1876-1880 and 1884-1911), who was fond of all things French, the empty square was paved and planted with trees;

fountains and benches were installed and a bandstand erected, all in a "French" fashion.

The trees in the Jardín, often mistakenly called Indian laurel, are actually breadnut trees (*brosimum alicastrum Swartz*), members of the Mulberry family, and native to tropical America. The trees can grow to 90 feet, but the ones in the Jardín are trimmed in a round shape with a flat top several times a year, apparently for aesthetic reasons. The breadnut tree can produce plum-like fruits up to an inch long and was an important food source for the Maya, but San Miguel is located too far north for the fruit to mature.

The covered and arched portales on the west and east side of the Jardín are called, respectively, *Portal Allende* and *Portal Guadalupe*.

The Jardín is the living room of the community, the place where the people have their shoes shined, pick up the newspaper, meet friends, trade gossip, listen to the mariachis, watch the dancers, buy snacks and toys. Children share benches with *ancianos*. The gringos tend to favor the southern side, facing the Parroquia, basking in the sun. Mexicans favor the shady spots. On Sunday evenings the *paseo* goes on till late evening when young men and women parade randomly around the plaza in a flirtatious charade.

The Parroquia is lit up on most evenings, and always during fiestas. The switch for the lights is located in the police station across the street and City Hall pays the electric bill.

A week or so before Christmas the bandstand in the center of the plaza is turned into a crèche, in the past often with live sheep, chickens, and a donkey.

The First Walk

We cross the esplanade to the atrium of the two churches.

Parroquia de San Miguel Arcángel It seems appropriate that we begin with the iconic *Parroquia de San Miguel Arcángel* which dominates the plaza. It is the "new" parish church (San Rafael, next door, with the clock tower, was the first). It is not a cathedral. It is not the oldest church in San Miguel. *"Parroquia"* simply means "parish." Its façade was only finished a little over 100 years ago.

The order for a new parish church construction came in 1682, to be built next to the old one, San Rafael. The architect, Marco Antonio Sobrarías, followed a typical model, a floor plan in the form of a cross, with small chapels on the sides and a great dome. The church was finished in the last years of the 17th century, although there was no bell tower yet. Two towers, one higher than the other, were eventually erected, the first in the early 1700s, the second not until 1740. Because of space constraints, this new church had to face north. San Rafael's footprint made it impossible to orient the new church toward the western valley, a more desirable vista.

In the 1750s and 60s the church was enlarged: another dome and an octagonal *camarín*, a chapel behind the main altar, were added as was a great vault underneath the church, a crypt where hundreds of clerics and important citizens are buried, among them the (twice) president of Mexico, Anastasio Bustamante. (See Notables, page 128.) The crypt is open to the public on November 2, the Day of the Dead.

By 1880 both towers were beginning to crumble and were demolished, paving the way for the construction of the façade of the Parroquia we see today. This was accomplished by Zeferino Gutiérrez, a local stone mason and architect who is usually described as an illiterate, indigenous maestro, inspired by postcard images of Gothic cathedrals in Europe but in fact was a gifted and experienced architect and builder who clearly had his own ideas. The result of his efforts is a mass of pink pilasters, balustrades, spires and steeples that soar over the grand houses that rim the Jardín.

The new façade of the church, only about 30 feet deep, was finished in 1888. Since then the church has become famous, its image widely reproduced in magazines and books, the subject of millions of snapshots by awed tourists. It is an icon that instantly identifies San Miguel the way the Eiffel Tower, say, announces Paris.

It has also been reviled by some critics who have referred to the façade as "grotesque gothesque," and "Disneyesque." The word "wedding-cake" has been invoked. The historian Francisco de la Maza was perhaps most blunt: "This famous façade … is an architectural error. It does not fit, in any way, with the San Miguel atmosphere and architecture. Besides, its crude construction does not have any of the grace and refinement that make the true gothic. Mr. Gutiérrez, overlooking tradition and lacking understanding of its meaning, disregarding the harmony of the whole, built his pseudo-gothic mass over the old, very Mexican 18th century church, destroying the colonial look of the plaza." But others have said kinder words. Wrote the travel writer Kate Simon: "Although it bears a wispy resemblance to the lace of Milan and Chartres, its lightly crazy style adds an appropriate touch, some say, to a town which has its other loony aspects." Stirling Dickinson insisted, "There is nothing quite like it anywhere in the world." The writer Robert Somerlott perhaps summed it up best: "The common people of the town love it, boast of it, and recall it with longing when they are away. That, perhaps, was the builder's finest achievement."

In the 1940s two new chapels were added to the church. The interiors of the church's chapels overall are a mishmash ranging from exquisite to abysmal. The font in the baptistery, for example, in the first chapel to the left, is remarkably beautiful, while murals in other side chapels are awful.

There is a much-revered treasure in the Parroquia. In the second side chapel on the left side of the church is a 16th century statue of *El Señor de la Conquista* (The Lord of the Conquest, the Conquest referring to religious conversion). This statue, made by Indians from Pátzcuaro from the heart of cornstalks mixed with the mucilage of orchid bulbs, is thus very light. It figures large in the Mass and fiesta of the same name celebrated on the first Friday in March, when Indian *concheros* dance for much of the day in the esplanade of the Parroquia. When the statue was being brought to San Miguel around 1575, the friars carrying it, Francisco Doncel and Pedro de Burgos, were murdered by Indians at a pass a few miles south of town, now called *El Puente del Fraile*. They were among the first martyrs in Mexico and were buried in the old Parroquia. The statue was eventually recovered.

Many examples of pagan forms have been transplanted into Mexican churches. There are dozens of Aztec religious symbols called *nauchampas* (The Four Directions of the Wind) on the outside walls of the Parroquia. The unusual transparency in the towers of the façade has been linked to allusions to Ehecatl, the Aztec God of the Four Winds.

We now walk to the eastern side of the atrium past the obelisk with the statue of Diez de Sollano y Dávalos, a native of San Miguel who was appointed bishop of León, the first Mexico-born cleric to reach that high office. He authorized the construction of the *Parroquia's* new façade and approved the plans. (See Notables, page 133.)

Iglesia de San Rafael (Santa Escuela de Cristo) San Rafael (also an archangel), the church with the clock, usually called *Santa Escuela*, is the oldest church in San Miguel and was first called *"El Templo de la Fundación."* It has been much modified. After the first settlement, San Miguel de los Chichimecas, was abandoned and the Villa de San Miguel was founded (1555), the parish was established in 1564 to instruct the natives in the Christian religion. Construction began in that year, authorized by the first bishop of Michoacán, Vasco de Quiroga. It was built of adobe, with a pitched roof and a small bell tower. The first documentation on construction does not appear until the 1570s and the church was still under construction in 1578, when an official regulation directed that Indians stealing cattle from Spaniards would be sentenced by the owners to labor

"for as long as they deemed fair, to work in the building of the church for the village of San Miguel in process at this time." It is not known when the building was finished, but by 1649 the church was already nearly in ruins, the bell tower collapsed. It had also become too small for the rapidly growing community. Plans were made for a new *parroquia*. San Rafael was eventually reconstructed after the new larger parish church was finished, and for a time was referred to as the *"Parroquia Vieja."* Before the new church was built, a small hospice ("a place where pilgrims could dwell, the ill could rest and be healed …") and a cemetery were located on Calle Hospicio behind the church.

After the construction of the new parish church, the old one was little used until it came to be the site of a religious school, *La Hermandad de la Santa Escuela de Cristo* (The Brotherhood of the Holy School of Christ), founded in 1742 by Father Luis Felipe Neri de Alfaro. (See Notables, page 126.) The church is still called Santa Escuela by most of the local people.

In 1762 the new bell tower was raised to accommodate a clock, a gift to San Miguel el Grande from the city of Madrid. (Soon after, the name Calle San Joaquín was changed to Calle Reloj—Clock Street, since the clock could be seen for much of its length.) In the 1890s the clock was removed and reinstalled at the newly-built Waterworks on Chorro. Ten years later, a new Swiss clock was inaugurated in the bell tower of Santa Escuela on September 16, 1901, Independence Day. (For an explanation of its sounds, see A Hundred Bells, page 117.)

Like its neighbor, Santa Escuela also lost part of its original tower to remodeling and received a new north-facing façade, also designed by Zeferino Gutiérrez and also executed in the neo-Gothic style of the church next door. But the western façade of the church was not changed and remains as the severe original with its small sculpture of Christ and a tiny medallion.

While the church is dark and gloomy, and the images of the suffering Christ tend to be seriously depressing, there is a small side chapel that is bright and cheerful. The funds for its construction were contributed by Zeferino Gutiérrez, who is buried there along with his family.

After leaving the atrium we turn right (east) on Calle Correo past a 100-year old market.

Mercado Aldama The one-story building to the left of Santa Escuela, now an open-air restaurant called La Terraza, was designed and built in 1901 by Zeferino Gutiérrez and became known for a time as *El Mercado de las Flores*, the Flower Market.

Across the street, we pass one of the oldest houses in the town.

La Casa Quemada The splendid yellow 18th century mansion on the southeast corner of the Jardín became known as *La Casa Quemada*, the Burnt House, for a great fire that in the 19th century raged through its halls. (A visitor, noting that the town has no fire hydrants, asked an elderly native, "What do you do if a fire breaks out?" The man pondered the question, then replied, "Mostly, *señor*, we remember it.") The building was the home of *Mariscal* (Marshall) Francisco Antonio de  Lanzagorta, who fought with the rebels during the early part of the War of Independence. He was captured and shot by Loyalist forces in Chihuahua on May 11, 1811.

Further in the block on our left we pass Correo 12, the site of the first post office late in the 18th century. On the right side of the doorway you can still see the original mail slot.

Oficina de Correos The new post office is the last building on the block; part of the building once housed a chapel used by Franciscan nuns. As with all Catholic Church real estate, the property was expropriated by the government in 1857.

Across the street, on the right-hand side of Calle Correo is a colonial building with an imposing facade.

Casa del Conde Jaral de Berrio at Correo 17 is a residence built in 1787 by the Spaniard Juan de Moncada, Count of Jaral de Berrio. The great door with its beautiful door knocker is usually open, affording a view of a colonial patio. After the Parroquia this door knocker is probably the most photographed subject in San Miguel.

Still facing east, the street on your left is one of the shortest streets in San Miguel, once called, what else, Calle Corta (Short Street) but renamed Corregidora after a famous Mexican heroine. (See Notables, page 137.) We continue walking east on Calle Correo for one block, past several large colonial homes to the next street, where we turn right on a narrow alley.

Callejón de los Chiquitos The Alley of the Little Ones is one of the prettiest streets in San Miguel, only one block long, with mostly small houses, although there are several bed and breakfast inns and a kindergarten school in the middle of the block.

At the end of the street we turn left on Calle Hospicio.

Calle Hospicio is actually part of a street that has many names. Several lower blocks of the street are named Pila Seca and Cuadrante, a common practice in San Miguel, and confusing to new visitors.

We turn right at the next corner on Calle Barranca, opposite the fountain, La Fuente de la Sirena, with its damaged Siren sculpture, scrupulously kept clean by a neighbor.

Calle Barranca Once a working-class neighborhood where many weavers made *rebozos*, some of the houses have been rehabilitated.

On the left in the next block at number 28 is the house where the War of Independence hero *Pípila* was born. We continue walking to the following block where the street changes names and is now called Calle Chorro. At the end of Calle Chorro on the left, up a few steps, we find one of the town's newer churches.

Templo de la Vera Cruz The Church of the True Cross was built in the 1890s. It is thought that this was the site where a small chapel was built or a cross planted when the mission in 1551 first moved up the hill from its original settlement in San Miguel Viejo. Nothing remains from those days. Although the Chorro spring was conveniently near, the location was not suitable for the growing community and the town was eventually laid out on a more level site down the hill. Beyond a small arch next to the church is a steep series of 160 steps leading to the Salida a Querétaro and *El Mirador*, one of the town's two overlooks.

We can now explore the many terraces and steps around the former Waterworks.

El Chorro, the Waterworks, and the Casa de la Cultura The spring called *El Chorro* (The Spurt or Jet) once supplied all the water for San Miguel. Pipes were connected to many private and public fountains. The Canal family donated money for the public baths and laundry early in the 19th century. Two larger basins were used as pools. The baths were improved and enlarged in 1901. There were seven separate chambers, "large enough to enjoy and exercise a bit." The baths, each with an identifying number, are no longer used and are now under the classrooms of the *Casa de la Cultura*, opened in 2000, a government-sponsored educational and cultural enterprise for adults and children offering instructions and workshops in music, painting, literature, and dance. One of the former baths is a small art gallery.

A traveler in 1908 wrote after arriving in San Miguel: "… instead of going to bed, leaving our luggage at the hotel, we headed toward the poetic baths, almost hidden among trees and flowers. The cold and crystal clear water of these baths practically relieved us from the fatigue of the journey … There is an abundance of water … a stream of clear water always flows down the streets of San Miguel and is ultimately used for irrigation of the orchards located down the hill." No longer. As the Independencia aquifer's water level lowered, *El Chorro* stopped producing around 1950. With more than 800 deep wells sunk in the municipio of San Miguel, (only 15 for drinking water in the city), about 100 in rural communities for potable water and nearly 700 wells used for industrial or agricultural purposes, the water level in the aquifer beneath the municipio has continued to fall, and thus the pressure and amount of water of the springs are diminished or eliminated.

From the *Casa de la Cultura* we walk down the hill. At the foot of the hill on the corner of Calle Recreo and Calle Santa Elena is the public laundry.

Los Lavaderos The free public laundry, a collection of 19 stone tubs used, especially on weekends, for washing clothes or sometimes children and pets. On Saturdays and Sundays local artists display their work in the adjacent patio.

At the bottom of Calle Santa Elena is one of five entrances to a park.

Parque Benito Juárez The park has been open to the public for more than 100 years. In 1904 Dr. Ignacio Hernández Macías, a physician, then mayor of San Miguel, proposed to use municipal funds to buy some three hectares (about

eight acres) of orchards for a park. The land was then at the edge of the town near the area known as Guadiana. There were no parks at that time in San Miguel. The proposal was enthusiastically received, properties were purchased and cobbled together, more than a thousand trees (mulberries, cedars and walnut) were planted, and a park was born.

Originally named *Parque Joaquín Obregón González*, after a San Miguel native and a popular governor of Guanajuato for 18 years, the name was changed in 1916 to "Benito Juárez," after the beloved Indian president. The park straddles a small arroyo that issues from the Valle del Maíz. It was sometimes called "French Park" while the Francophile Porfirio Díaz was president and for some years there was a French-style bandstand in the middle of the park. On Sunday afternoons concerts were offered to the citizens of San Miguel who brought their own chairs to these musical matinees.

In the 1940s and 1950s the famous Mexican opera singer José Mojica lived in a house adjoining the park, now the hotel Villa Santa Mónica. (In 2007 the street bordering the park on the south was renamed after the singer.) The park is frequented by joggers and strollers; there are several basketball courts, a picnic area, fountains, rest rooms, a bandstand, and a pleasant playground for children with see-saws, slides, and swings.

For about ten days, beginning on Candelaria Day, February 2, much of the park is transformed into a huge colorful garden when many nurseries from all over Mexico bring plants, pots, and flowers for display and sale.

After exploring the park we head for the northwest corner and walk up Calle Aldama north toward the Jardín.

Calle Aldama (it has had many different names) is one of the oldest in San Miguel. The view straight ahead, the back of the *Parroquia*, reveals the second dome that was added to the church in the early 1760s.

At the end of two blocks we cross Calle Cuadrante, pass by the fountain, jog to the left and then the right and walk up the gently curving Cuna de Allende (Cradle of Allende).

Cuna de Allende The house on the left at No. 5 was built by the then mayor Miguel María Malo between 1782-1784. Don Miguel founded the regiment of the Dragoons of the Queen that became the military core group at the outbreak of the War of Independence. His son, Luis Malo, born in this house, was an Independence War hero. He was caught by Loyalist forces and executed in Monclova in 1811. The building is now a hotel and restaurant. Another restaurant on the right in the middle of the block was originally a chapel, part of the *Parroquia*.

A short distance ahead on the right at the end of the street is a monument to Fray Juan de San Miguel, the founder of the city.

Statue of Fray Juan de San Miguel To the right of the church, on the corner of Cuna de Allende is a statue of Fray Juan de San Miguel consoling an Indian. (See Notables, page 135.) It was dedicated in 1942 on the 400th anniversary of the founding of San Miguel.

On the opposite corner is the ancestral home of Ignacio de Allende, now a museum.

Museo Histórico de San Miguel de Allende The museum is the birthplace of the great Mexican patriot, Ignacio Allende y Unzaga. (See Notables, page 126.) The house was a wedding present from his father to his mother. Construction was begun in 1764 and the mansion occupied several years later. A Latin inscription above the front door reads *"Hic natus ubique notus,"* which translates as "Born here, known everywhere." The house is one of the finest examples of 18th century colonial architecture in San Miguel, a beautifully proportioned, graceful dwelling in a neoclassical design with some baroque decorations in the form of grapes, flowers, and leaves.

From 1919-1979 the lower level was occupied by a small general store and an apothecary. The building was bought by the State of Guanajuato, restored and opened as the *Museo Casa de Allende* in 1985. In 2007 a total renovation was begun and in the spring of 2009 the museum, renamed *Museo Histórico de San Miguel de Allende*, was reopened in time for the Centennial and Bicentennial Celebrations. The first floor of the museum presents exhibits that highlight Allende's role at the beginning of the War of Independence and include many video displays offering information about the town of San Miguel, its founding, and important events in its history. The second floor features a recreation of Allende's home, including bedrooms, kitchen, and chapel, much of it furnished with original items from collections of other Mexican museums.

Admission is free on Sundays but, like most museums in Mexico, it is closed on Mondays.

The Second Walk

The second walk also both departs and returns to the *Jardín*, but visits a different part of town.

We begin our walk on the north side of the *Jardín*. Two buildings are of historic interest:

Palacio Municipal In the middle of the block is the former City Hall, the *Ex-Presidencia*. The building was constructed in 1736, around the time when this area became the main plaza. Over the centuries there have been several fires and the building has been modified a number of times. Little of the original remains. A short time after the struggle for independence began in 1810, the archives were plundered and burned. The *Presidencia* was the site of the formation of Mexico's first independent city council, on September 17, 1810. During the Revolution, in 1911, a mob burned the building, destroying much of the archives again. The building now houses a small exhibit space, the tourist office and a police sub-station. In 2005 a new City Hall was built on the outskirts of town on the road to Querétaro.

Another important site is the last building, on the corner of Calle Reloj.

Casa de las Conspiraciones The House of Conspiracies, on the corner of Reloj and the *Plaza Principal* was built in the middle of the 18th century by Ignacio Allende's father and later owned by Domingo Allende, one of his brothers. Early in the 19th century secret meetings were held here and plans made to fight for independence against the Viceroyalty. A sign on the side of the building announces "*Aquí se fraguó la independencia de Nueva España*" (The independence of New Spain was forged here). It reads further: "In the mezzanine of this house, disguised as dances that took place in the living room, Don Ignacio Allende and the people involved gathered to talk about the adequate means to achieve the independence of the nation."

The house on the opposite corner of Calle Reloj and the street now called Calle San Francisco, once a store called La Princesa owned by Francisco José Landeta, was sacked by the insurgents in 1810. It is now a bar and office.

The house across the street on the corner of San Francisco and the Portal Guadalupe was owned by Domingo de Berrio, a Spaniard and city counselor. He was imprisoned during the rebel attack in 1810 and transported with the insurgents but died during the siege of the Granary in Guanajuato two weeks later.

We continue walking east on Calle San Francisco until we come almost to the end of the first block.

Templo de la Tercera Orden, one of the oldest churches in San Miguel. The church, first named after San Antonio (since it abutted the San Antonio monastery), eventually came to be run by Franciscans. Construction was started early in the 17th century, but stopped in 1638 for lack of funds, started again in 1680 and the church was finally dedicated in 1713 after the belfry and main altar were finished. Small, simple and austere, with a huge flying buttress on its south side, the church is crowned by a slender and handsome angular steeple with a small bell. One critic described its architecture as "poor, simple and strong." A statue of St. Francis stands in a niche above the front door, which displays several carved wooden panels bearing the symbols of the Franciscan Order, the crossed arm of God, bare and white, and the arm of a Franciscan monk, robed and brown. On the southern (lateral) façade is a vaulted niche with an image of San Diego, the patron saint of Spain, while above it is displayed a huge cross of Lorraine (with its twin cross-pieces), the cross favored by the Franciscans. Gentlemen could join the Third Order and take the vows of monks, but it was not binding: they could go out into the world for business or pleasure. The vows were neither permanent nor final. They also had the privilege of being buried in clerical garb.

The monastery behind the church of the Third Order is not open to the public.

Convento de San Francisco A monastery (or "convent," the words were used interchangeably) was possibly first built in the last decade of the 1500s and run by members of the Order of San Antonio, but nothing remains from that time. In the next century Franciscan missionaries, aided by their Indian converts, set out to build another convent. (Thus early in the history of San Miguel Calle San Francisco was called "Calle San Antonio.") Nothing remains of that effort. The structure was rebuilt and much modified in the 18th century. During the Revolution the building was used as an army barracks and stable.

At the head of a tiny park is a church that was built in the late 1700s on the site of an older, smaller church.

Iglesia de San Francisco The San Francisco church is still sometimes referred to as the "Spanish church," to distinguish it from the "Indian church"

(the Oratorio). Built during the last two decades of the 18th century, the church represents two completely different architectural philosophies. The elaborate baroque façade, probably designed by the gifted Lorenzo Rodríguez stands in great contrast with the stark base of the tower. The construction of the San Francisco church began in 1779 with a 2,000-peso stake (then a small fortune) apparently won in a lottery. Wealthy families donated monies, and other funds were raised through assessments on bullfight tickets. The first stone of the church was laid on June 29, 1779.

There are two façades, but it is the south-facing one that has inspired comments ranging from "wonderful" to "mad" to "insane" to "magnificent." It is all of those. It is lavishly ornamented in the Churrigueresque style. José Churriguera, a Spanish architect and sculptor, nearly outdid the baroque, and this façade contains some of the finest, graceful *estípites* (pilasters in the shape of truncated, inverted obelisks) and a collection of famous saints of the Franciscan Order, as well as flowers, cherubs, vines, and virgins. A statue of St. Francis crowns the façade and looks down on it all, while the image of the crucified Christ is displayed somewhat lower, above a stained-glass window, and flanked by representations of Our Lady of Sorrows and of St. John. The dome of the church is covered in blue and white tiles.

The three-section bell tower as well as the dome and the interior was probably designed and built many years later by Francisco Eduardo Tresguerras, the leading architect of the region, using a neoclassical style that harmoniously integrates with the rest of the building. The highest sections of the tower are octagonal. Construction was finished on April 13, 1799. Originally the statues of eight Franciscan saints were installed, but only seven remain (in 1943 lightning toppled one of the statues).

The interior of the church is spacious and quite beautiful, but as different from the glorious exterior as the central façade is from its flanking walls. A small tile on

the side of the entrance says *"Convento de San Antonio,"* confusing many visitors. It refers to the old convent behind the church, first named after San Antonio.

On the southeast corner of the Plazuela San Francisco is a small statue of Cristóbal Colón, Christopher Columbus. On October 12, his connection with the Americas is celebrated as the *Día de la Raza* in Mexico. Across Calle Juárez, on the corner of Calle San Francisco, stands a former stage-coach inn.

Casa de las Postas The inn, sometimes also named *"Casa de las Diligencias"* (House of the Carriages), was used by wealthy travelers and as a place to change horses. The handsome building now houses several offices and stores. The old coach entrance is around the corner. It was one of many inns that served the "Silver Route" between Zacatecas and Mexico City.

We walk left (north) onto Calle Juárez and walk past the side entrance of the San Francisco church to the corner of Juárez and Mesones. The (no longer functioning) gasoline pump on the corner, said to be the first installed in San Miguel in 1943, has become a much photographed icon. We cross the street and take a slight jog to the left then right into another short street called Pepe Llanos. Ahead is the "Indian" church.

Oratorio de San Felipe Neri y Santa Casa de Loreto In 1714 the Oratorio de San Felipe Neri replaced an older chapel called Ecce Homo that had been built in 1628, almost 100 years earlier, by a lay brotherhood called *Cofradía de Mulatos*. African slaves and the offspring of their unions with Indians had been an important part of the workforce since the late 1500s and were frequently employed in the textile mills and other enterprises in San Miguel. These mulattos (from *mula*, mule) perhaps constituted a third of the population.

The Oratorio was built at the urging of Juan Antonio Pérez de Espinosa, a priest from Pátzcuaro, who in 1712 had been invited to deliver several sermons in San Miguel, and who had, as many have since, fallen in love with the town. (His statue is in the atrium of the church.) The people loved his sermons and his personality and asked that he move to San Miguel and establish a community of the Order of San Felipe Neri. It was decided that the Ecce Homo church, known as the "mulatto" church, would be the preferred site. The mulattos were reluctant to permit a rebuilding and argued that the building had been erected with their own labor and monies, but they were defeated in the legal battle that ensued. (As late as the 1740s there were mulatto riots involving the legal status of the church.)

The building was finished in 1714 but has been modified many times.

Eventually the name Ecce Homo fell into disuse and the new church came to be called simply the *Oratorio*. It was named after the first *Oratorio* built by the Italian saint in Rome in the 1560s. The musical form known as oratorio developed from the significance given to music in Neri's church services. The dictionary defines "*oratorio*" as "an extended musical composition." (Handel's "The Messiah" is an *oratorio*.)

The façade is a beautiful example of baroque architecture and superb workmanship. Five niches in the façade of the church shelter statues of St. Peter, St. Paul, St. Joseph, St. John the Baptist, and, of course, St. Felipe Neri.

The original entrance to Ecce Homo, along with a small sculpture of *La Virgen de la Soledad*, was retained on the east side of the new building and can be seen by entering the small courtyard to the right of the church.

In the left transept of the Oratorio is the chapel of the Virgin of Loreto, who was the patron saint of the wealthy Canal family.

Santa Casa de Loreto In 1735 Don Manuel Tómas de la Canal funded the construction of the *Santa Casa* (Holy House) chapel. The cost was 36,000 pesos, an extraordinary amount of money at that time. It is a replica of the famous Santa Casa in Loreto, Italy, which is said to be the original home of the Virgin Mary in Nazareth. When "Infidels" captured the Holy Land, so the story goes, the house of the Virgin Mary was desecrated. This so exasperated the angels that one night, under command of St. Michael, they lifted the house from its founda-

tion and moved it to Italy. (The Virgin of Loreto is the patron saint of aviators!) The story is an "authorized" legend of the Church: the faithful are urged, but not required, to believe it. An inscription at the entrance of the Santa Casa informs us that "This is the house in which the Son of God was conceived."

The Holy House comprises two spaces: The first, called the Living Room, facing the transept of the Oratorio is the chapel itself with the image of the Virgin of Loreto on the altar. A small eight-sided chamber, a *camarín*, with a richly decorated dome ceiling is reached by way of two narrow lateral hallways. It is the Bedroom. This inner sanctum is only open by special appointment and on September 8, the Virgin's day.

Glazed tiles from Puebla, Spain, and China cover the floors and lower friezes of the walls. The walls are covered with fine gold cloth. The ornamentation is astonishing. There are many altars and paintings devoted to or dedicated to saints.

The octagonal *camarín* has six altars. The donors, Don Manuel and his wife Doña María, are depicted in stone niches on either side of the room. They are buried under the floor of the Living Room. This is the most sumptuous religious building in San Miguel and another example of the exuberant baroque style that flourished during the 18th century.

After leaving the atrium of the Oratorio, we turn left past the fountain toward the plaza.

Templo de Nuestra Señora de la Salud A short distance along the northern edge of the Plaza Cívica is the baroque Church of Our Lady of Health. Construction was begun early in the 18th century but soon suspended for a lack of funds. It was not finished until 1734 after Father Luis Felipe Neri Alfaro invested a large part of his inheritance. It became the chapel for the Colegio de San Francisco de Sales, which adjoins the church.

The building is surmounted with an enormous scallop shell, a motif common to neoclassicism and seen often in San Miguel architecture. The dome of the church is composed of multi-hued tiles, while the pink lantern of the dome has suggested to many the form of the *tuna* (prickly pear), the fruit of the nopal cactus.

The interior is small and charming. A tiny shrine on the left side of the church is devoted to *Santo Niño de la Salud* (Holy Child of Health). Toys, pictures,

and discarded plaster casts are displayed to show gratitude for the cures of children's ailments. The space on the right is dedicated to the *Virgen de la Salud*. At the top of the corner dome supports are paintings of four females representing Prudence, Temperance, Fortitude, and Justice. On November 22, the Day of St. Cecilia, the patron saint of musicians and the blind, many musicians come to the church to serenade her.

Next to the church (toward the east) is the Colegio de San Francisco de Sales.

Colegio de San Francisco de Sales The clergy at the Oratorio church asked permission to build a school where students would be taught "Grammar, Rhetoric, Philosophy, and Scholastic and Moral Theology, with such a level of quality that those attending would be allowed to graduate from [the University of Mexico]." The request to build the "Illustrious and Royal College of San Francisco de Sales" was approved by the king of Spain in 1734, but construction was not begun until 1753. The school attracted famous scholars, among them Dr. Juan Benito Díaz Gamarra y Dávalos, born in 1745, who became dean of the school. He had entered the priesthood at age nineteen, obtained a Ph.D. from the University of Pisa, published many books, and lived and taught the last decade of his life in San Miguel. He died in 1783 at age 38.

The College became even more important after the expulsion of the Jesuits in 1767. Since the Jesuits were New Spain's important educators, their absence was a great blow to thought. But in San Miguel, wrote Robert Somerlott, "the intellectual light was kept burning, a somewhat lonely flame at the time." The college was possibly attended by Allende (although there is no record of his graduating), the Aldama brothers, and Juan Umarán, all heroes of the War of Independence, as well as Carlos Montes de Oca, the first governor of Guanajuato, and Díez de Sollano, the first bishop of León. The school suffered damage during the War of Independence. When the insurgents entered San Miguel late in the day of September 16, 1810, Ignacio Allende jailed the Spanish citizens in the Colegio to protect them from the mob.

The building, now privately owned, was at times used as a store. Abandoned for many years it was restored in 1998 and is now occupied by a branch of the University of León.

When you enter the Plaza Cívica and walk the adjoining streets, Mesones and Colegio, you have entered a very different world. An open space dominated by a statue of Allende on a horse, the plaza is a blend of religion, commerce, and antiquity.

Plaza Cívica Generalisimo Ignacio Allende, first called the *Plaza de la Soledad*, was the main plaza of San Miguel from 1555 to 1737. The plaza became too small for the rapidly growing population of San Miguel el Grande. And so the larger, empty space in front of the two parish churches, old and new, became the new Plaza Principal, eventually called the *Jardín*.

In 1889 the Plaza de la Soledad became the location of the first *Mercado Municipal Ignacio Ramírez*, a large covered market designed and built by Zeferino Gutiérrez. During 1969, the Year of Allende, the bicentennial of Allende's birth, the building was torn down after a disastrous fire. The plaza was redesigned, repaved, trees planted and the general's equestrian statue unveiled. A new market was built behind the Colegio de San Francisco de Sales. The plaza was renamed Plaza Cívica. It is a favorite of Mexicans, with popular churches and stores nearby. It is often the venue for concerts and fairs.

Calle Mesones The street that borders the Plaza on the south, Calle Mesones, is named after the inns that once lined the street and were used by the mule skinners and tradesmen who traveled back and forth along the Silver Route. There were probably a half-dozen hostelries. Little is left today to indicate their original use, except for their large entryways. The Mesón de San José, at Mesones 38 (but with the number 19 above the door!) and the Mesón de San Sebastián further east down the block, were among the largest.

After meandering around the Plaza we walk around the corner and turn left (north) on Calle Colegio. The covered market is ahead on the left.

Mercado Municipal Ignacio Ramírez You can explore the myriad stalls offering everything from fruit to flowers to shoes to tasty *tacos* and *burritos*. The market was built in 1969, after the old market of the same name, which occupied much of the Plaza Cívica, was demolished. The new market is open seven days a week.

Behind and next to the covered market is the Artisans Market.

Mercado de Artesanías follows a meandering 1,500-foot long narrow alley called *Andador* (Walkway) Lucas Balderas, named after a local war hero. The *Andador* is lined with dozens of stands displaying an astonishing variety of artisan's products, from fine silver jewelry to knick-knacks.

We follow the *Andador* to the first cross-street, Calle Loreto, where we turn left (one could keep going for two more blocks). At the next intersection, Calle Loreto and Calle Insurgentes, we turn right to the yellow Santa Ana church on the corner of Insurgentes and Reloj.

Templo de Nuestra Señora de Santa Ana The church, a boxy edifice with seven sturdy buttresses, was built in 1847 after an earlier church was torn down. The church underwent a major restoration in 2001-2002.

The church has no bell tower, but on the west side there is a small *espadaña*, a belfry from which three bells are suspended.

Next door to the church on Calle Insurgentes is the Library.

Biblioteca Pública If the Jardín is the town's "living room," this is the town's "den." More than a public library, it is the city's center for education and culture, offering space for bilingual study, research, discussions, films, lectures, concerts, and theater.

In 1954 a Canadian expatriate, Helen Wale, invited Mexican children in her neighborhood to peruse the many magazines she had in her home. The activity became popular and so, as the number of young visitors grew, she installed chairs and activity tables for the children. Several other expats began to offer assistance. The space soon was inadequate and the following year Mrs. Wale and her volunteer collaborators decided to rent a building to house a children's library, which they supplemented with educational materials. As Helen Wale's little library became more popular, the expat volunteers asked the state governor for a space to establish a library that would serve the entire community. In 1958 a building that had been used as the city's slaughterhouse was leased to the non-profit civil association known as the Biblioteca Pública de San Miguel de Allende, A.C. The *Biblioteca* also has a more ancient history.

In 1734 a group of priests from the nearby Oratorio church founded a community house for poor women who were single, widowed, or abandoned by their husbands, a sort of combination of orphanage and convent. Called "*El Colegio y Recogimiento de las Matronas y Doncellas de Nuestra Señora Santa Ana*," it was "a *Beaterio*, a School and Cloister for Women and Maidens." After the government expropriated church properties during the War of Reform and closed the convents, the building was left in ruins. Early in the 20th century it became the city's slaughterhouse. Over the years many renovations and changes have been made.

To help offset expenses, one of the first programs created was the House and Garden Tour, now a San Miguel tradition conducted at noon every Sunday except Easter and certain other holidays. More than 250 homes are in the inventory and usually three houses are featured each week. Proceeds from the tour benefit the library's many educational programs for children and each year help provide more than 100 scholarships for high school and university students.

In 1975 the Biblioteca launched a weekly English-language newspaper. It was called "This Week in San Miguel" and consisted of four pages. Soon after renamed "Atención San Miguel," the publication steadily grew. By 2009 it had a circulation of 3,000, averaged 120 pages per issue, and had become the single most important source of revenue to the Library. In 1982 a Rural Libraries Program was started that has supplied hundreds of rural communities with bookshelves and books.

With more than 50,000 volumes in English and Spanish, it is one of the largest public libraries in Mexico. Run by a paid staff of about 50 people assisted by dozens of volunteers, the Library is visited by more than 500 adults and children daily.

There is an 85-seat theater, a café and restaurant, a gift shop, and several reading rooms including the Sala Quetzal. The Sala is the site of a distinguished mural depicting the Aztec God Quetzalcoatl on all four walls nearly floor to ceiling. The room also contains a significant Latin American collection of books and other works. The library offers art classes for children as well as conversational Spanish sessions. Every Thursday a flea market is conducted. Including film screenings, plays, lectures, and musical performances, the Library hosts more than 1,500 cultural activities each year.

Leaving the Library, we turn right toward the next intersection and there turn left on Calle Hidalgo. We turn right again at the next street, Calle Mesones. On the left at the end of the block is the city's charming and popular theater.

Teatro Ángela Peralta Construction of the theater was begun in 1871 with monies from the municipality and from private donations. Built "with adobe walls and a tile roof," it was finished in 1873. It was named after the soprano Ángela Peralta (see Notables, page 138) who was asked to give the inaugural performance. In 1886 some repairs and changes were made, a tin roof installed, but it wasn't until 1915 that the modest adobe structure was extensively remodeled and the handsome neoclassical façade added.

In the 1960s the theater fell on bad times, becoming a third-run movie house, "notorious for its stifling atmosphere, collapsing seats, and objects tossed from the balcony." When the film operation moved (to the Cine Aldama on San Francisco, the former home of the Aldama brothers), several attempts were made to restore the building. The theater was closed for many years, but reopened in 1975. In the last several decades many improvements have been made and the building continues to be the choice venue for concerts and other performances.

A half block south from the corner of the theater, across the street on Calle Hernández Macías, is the ex-convent now known as Bellas Artes.

Centro Cultural Ignacio Ramírez "El Nigromante" is almost always called *Bellas Artes* (Fine Arts). It was once part of a larger complex that included the La Concepción church behind the convent.

Both church and convent were partially financed by María Josefa Lina de  la Canal (see Notables, page 130), the oldest daughter of Manuel Tomás de la Canal and María de Hervás y Flores, who had inherited a fortune when her parents died (within a few days of each other). Plans and permits for the construction were begun in 1752, the Royal Decree to proceed was signed by King Ferdinand VI in 1754, and construction begun the following year.

The convent was to be the home for six dozen *Conceptionista* nuns; an early critic of the convent pronounced it "imprudently large" for such a small group. The architect was Francisco Martínez Gudiño, who also contributed to the building of several famous churches in Querétaro. The first part of the complex was occupied by the Order in December 1765, although it was far from complete. The benefactress, now Sor Josefa, spent only five years in the convent. She died in 1770 and was buried in the church beneath the choir. Much work was left unfinished for decades, since the inheritance monies were woefully inadequate. It would be 1842 before the convent was finished.

When in 1857 Church property was confiscated and convents closed during the Benito Juárez presidency, the convent became part of Mexico's federal holdings. In the first decade of the 20th century the building was used as a public elementary school. After the Revolution began in 1910, the building housed an Army cavalry regiment. In 1937 President Lázaro Cárdenas leased the building to Felipe Cossío del Pomar and evicted the garrison. The building was rehabilitated and became San Miguel's first private art school: *Escuela Universitaria de Bellas Artes*. In 1967 the ex-convent became part of Mexico's federal Fine Arts Institution and was renamed Centro Cultural Ignacio Ramírez "El Nigromante" after one of Mexico's great intellectuals, who was born only a block away. (See Notables, page 139.)

The courtyard has been called "magnificent, probably the most ambitious conventual undertaking in the country." The lower level features several galleries, an outdoor café and the nun's former dining room, with its unfinished mural painted by David Alfaro Siqueiros and several of his students in 1948, named "Vida y Obra del General Ignacio Allende," (Life and Works of General Ignacio Allende). There are other murals in the building: "The Pulque Tavern," "The Vampire Bat," and "The Weavers" by Pedro Martínez, and "The Washerwomen" by Eleanor Cohen. The upper level contains workshops and classrooms and the 300-seat Miguel Malo auditorium.

After leaving Bellas Artes we turn right (south) and enter the atrium of the church next door.

Iglesia y Convento de la Concepción A small nunnery is still located behind the church and the complex is always called *Las Monjas* (The Nuns). Near the end of the atrium is the entrance to the church. Construction of the church (and convent) was started in 1755 but the construction was not totally finished until more than 100 years later. The bell tower was not finished until 1842. The base of the cupola had been set in 1841, but it wasn't until 1891 that the dome was completed by Zeferino Gutiérrez shortly after he finished the new façade of the Parroquia. Almost a copy of the dome of *Eglise des Invalides* in Paris, it is ornamented with pairs of Corinthian columns on the lower level and with a balustrade and statues of saints on the upper level. A statue of the Immaculate Conception was placed on top and other carved saints surround the base of the dome.

The church is large, somber and austere, but with many admirable details: the gilded altar piece in the lower choir, polychrome sculptures of St. Joseph and the Immaculate Conception, and a number of paintings, including several by Miguel Antonio Martínez de Pocasangre, the creator of the murals at Atotonilco.

After leaving the church we walk east on Calle Canal back toward the *Jardín*. The glorious building on the right at the corner of the Jardín was the home of the Canal family.

Casa de la Canal The building on the corner of the Jardín and Calle Canal is the Casa del Mayorazgo de la Canal, sometimes misnamed the "Canal Palace."

Begun by Narciso Loreto de la Canal y Landeta, a grandson of Don Manuel Tomás de la Canal and finished by his son José Mariano in 1795, it is now a bank. It is an imposing example of an aristocratic residence in the neo-classical style with small and charming touches of baroque influence. The elaborately carved door on the side of the building on Calle Canal, one of the largest in San Miguel, is probably the most photographed doorway in San Miguel. Above the huge door is a niche containing the image of Our Lady of Loreto, the patron saint of the Canal family. The lambrequins and spandrels of the balconies that face the plaza are decorated with animal-shape elements.

The poet Rafael Solana nearly swooned, verbally, over the mansion:

> *It is, to me, the most important monument of civil architecture in San Miguel de Allende, and I believe it to be one of the soundest and more complete examples of colonial art in the country. Not many other constructions will so accurately blend grandeur and good taste. The sumptuous proportions throughout the building are only hindered by elegance. There is a dangerous balance between majesty and grace in its contour, so much so that although the construction seems grandiose, it is never arrogant or distasteful. The rich doorway and the fine courtyard are, undoubtedly, an example of the highest artistic value in the architectural treasures of the Colony.*

As we turn the corner we enter into the Portal de Allende, the covered arcade on the south side of the Jardín. It is very common in Mexico for even the most sumptuous buildings to have shops and businesses on the lower level, both for the convenience of the citizens and as an additional source of tax revenue.

We are back in the Jardín, but there is an abundance of other sights to discover and enjoy in San Miguel. The next section features more than a dozen of the treasures.

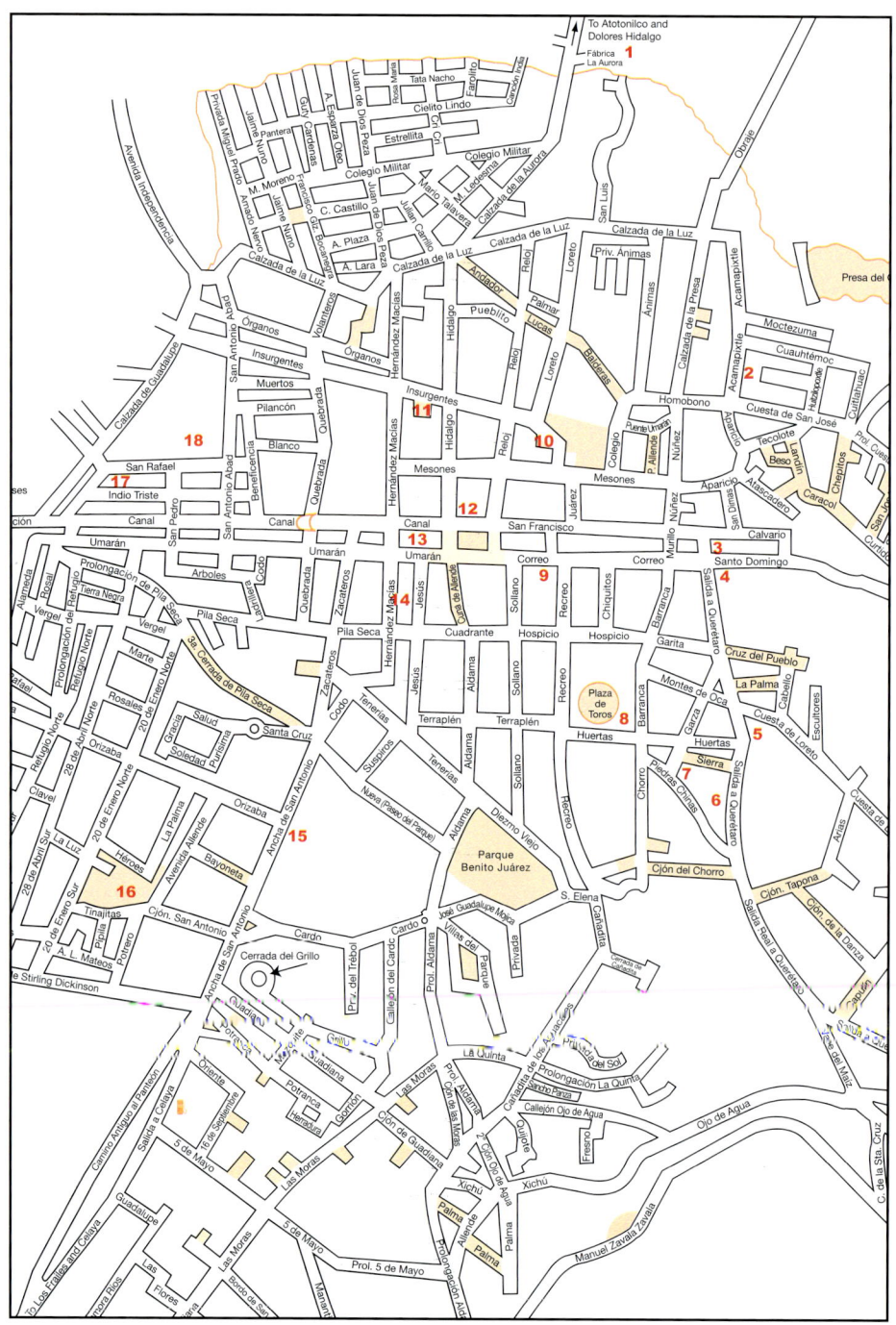

Other Interesting Sights

Fábrica La Aurora (1) is an art and design center that has in a few years become an important part of San Miguel's art scene. A little more than half a mile from the *Jardín*, La Aurora features dozens of artists' studios and galleries, all housed in an abandoned textile mill.

The mill, built in 1902, became a leading manufacturer of *manta* (unbleached cotton muslin) and was still San Miguel's largest employer, with more than 300 workers, when its well-known steam whistle blew for the last time on March 11, 1991. Increased foreign competition had brought many difficulties to the Mexican textile industry, and *Fábrica La Aurora* was no exception.

While maintaining its original façade and structure, large open spaces once filled with spindles and looms for making thread and weaving cloth were transformed into designer showrooms, artist's studios, and antique shops. Nearly four dozen tenants flourish in this unusual environment, and artists can often be found working in their studios. A restaurant, an outdoor café, a wine bar, and a bookstore are also on the premises.

La Otra Cara de México, The Other Face of Mexico (2), the small, private museum and gallery known as the Mask Museum, is located off the  Cuesta de San José. More than 500 Mexican ceremonial masks are on display in a handsomely curated environment. All the masks have been danced in indigenous ceremonies. The museum is open by appointment only by calling 154-4324 or via e-mail: info@casadelacuesta.com. A small donation to a charitable organization is requested.

Calvario (3) At the top of Calle San Francisco is the *Capilla de Nuestra Señora de Soledad*, called *Calvario* or sometimes *Calvarito*. San Miguel's Way of Fourteen Stations of the Cross (*Via Crucis*) ends at the chapel. *Calvario* is the Spanish word for "Calvary," the hill outside Jerusalem where the crucifixion of Jesus Christ took place.

Templo de Santo Domingo (4) The Santo Domingo church sits on a hill, called *Cerro de la Cruz*, at the top of Calle Correo. The church was consecrated in 1737 as the *Santuario de Guadalupe*. When the Dominican Order assumed its support, the name was changed to Santo Domingo. The *espadaña*, the belfry, appears to have four bells, but there are actually five: one part of the belfry is oriented toward the north.

La Ermita (5) The tiny chapel of *La Ermita* (The Hermitage) on the corner of the Salida a Querétaro and the Cuesta de Loreto was built in the middle of the 18th century, but the present façade and tower are of much more recent vintage. A stone stairway with a neoclassical façade was added in the 1870s by Zeferino Gutiérrez. It is sometimes called *La Capilla de la Virgen de Loreto* because a statue of the saint, brought from Europe, was kept in this chapel for a short time before being placed in the Santa Casa de Loreto in the Oratorio.

El Mirador (6) High above the city, on the Salida a Querétaro, is a popular overlook. Much of the city, the presa, the valley, and mountains beyond can be seen for miles around. The oversized bust at the site of the Mirador is of Pedro Vargas, whose house bookends the overlook.

Oratorio de los Siete Dolores de la Santísima Virgen (7) The small chapel on Calle Piedras Chinas, said to have been built in the late 1800s by Zeferino Gutiérrez, was abandoned for years but in the late 1990s was rehabilitated. Mass is regularly celebrated on Sunday mornings.

Plaza de Toros Oriente (8) Behind a huge red door on Call Recreo 52, in the middle of San Miguel de Allende, is hidden a 3,000-seat bullring. It is not visible from the street since it is located inside a block bordered by the streets of Hospicio, Recreo, Huertas, and Barranca. It is called the *Plaza de Toros Oriente*, the Eastern Bullring, because another older ring had been once located behind the Plaza Cívica. (There are more than 300 public bullrings in Mexico. The largest in the world is the 50,000-seat Plaza México ring in Mexico City. A bullfight is always called a *fiesta brava* or *corrida de toros*.)

Bullfighting was introduced by the Spanish conquistadores. In San Miguel el Grande in the 17th and early 18th centuries, bullfights were held in the *Plaza de Armas*, now called the *Jardín*, then a dusty open parade ground. Permission was granted to the Indians so they could celebrate the day of their patron saint, San Miguel Arcángel, with bullfights morning and evening. "The natives, "wrote one

chronicler, "guided by their landowners, would close up the plaza with makeshift fences in order to fight the wild bulls purchased in nearby haciendas … Initially amusement for the locals alone, the celebration soon turned into a noisy fair offering comedy, gambling, cockfights, public dances, and other attractions to lure vistors from the remotest places in the region."

Built in a centuries-old orchard called El Rosal that had become surrounded by new construction, the date of the current ring's construction is not known but it was probably begun in the 1850s. In the early 1940s, with the 400th anniversary of the founding of San Miguel rapidly approaching, the bullring was in a state of disrepair. Although only the dilapidated grandstand remained, along with crumbling stairways and piles of rocks that had once been sturdy walls, Felipe Cossío del Pomar nevertheless bought the property for 2,000 pesos (about 700 dollars at the time). When the anniversary activities started in September 1942, the bullring had been repaited and restored. Cossío wrote, "The Plaza de Toros boasted a comfortable grandstand crowned with a series of arches that covered the boxes under a classic *mozárabe* [Spanish-Moorish style] roof. Ring side seats, barriers along the walls of the ring for the bullfighter's refuge, and holding corrals with thick iron rings for the bulls completed the Plaza's very taurean image, reminiscent of the bullring in Ronda, Spain." The enterprise was an economic failure but during the celebrations Cossío del Pomar was named an adoptive son of San Miguel by the grateful community.

Bullfights are held irregularly a few dozen times a year; one of the most important takes place during the fiesta of San Miguel's patron saint in late September or early October. A billboard near the entrance on Recreo announces the dates of the bullfights along with the names of the matadors. The bullring can also be rented for special events, including weddings and exhibits. From time to time horse dressage shows are held, as are "bloodless" bullfights.

Casa del Conde de Loja (9) Francisco José de Landeta, a friend of Tomás de la Canal (and godfather to Canal's first child, María Josefa), who was already rich, married the daughter of another wealthy family from Querétaro. With the combined fortune, Landeta acquired a noble title, thus becoming the Count of the House of Loja. He built the mansion, which once occupied most of the first block on Sollano, in the mid-1700s. The street became known then as *Calle del Conde*. Only the elaborate entrance remains of the original building. The coat of arms of half a dozen noble families is shown above the doorway. The property now houses, among other enterprises, the local radio station and a travel agency. Across the street is the little Fountain of the Count, spouting water through pursed lips. A small door, said to allow access to the water from a convent that once occupied that building, is found on the back wall of the fountain.

Plazuela Zaragoza (10) A triangular space on the corner of Mesones and Pepe Llanos, where many of the buses stop, was once called San Felipe Neri but popularly called *La Rinconada*, The Little Corner. It is now known as Plaza Zaragoza, after Ignacio Zaragoza, the general who won the Battle of Puebla on May 5, 1862.

Plazuela San Felipe (11) Two blocks west on Calle Insurgentes is the Plazuela San Felipe, a tiny and charming rectangular park with benches and a fountain and surrounded by a half dozen *puestos* selling food and drinks.

El Arca de Noé (12) Noah's Ark, on the first block of Reloj was constructed by Isaac Cohen, a merchant born in Syria, who emigrated to Mexico in the 1920s. His business prospered and in 1942 he decided to build a structure dedicated to Noah. The six balconies on the front of the building are supported by 18 small animal sculptures. Other sculptures of animals line the roof. "The effect," wrote Robert Somerlott, "is delightful madness."

Casa de los Perros (13) The house on Umarán 4 is called *La Casa de los Perros*, because the shelf under the main balcony is supported by several carved figures of dogs. The house was built by Juan Antonio de Umarán. His grandson, Juan de Umarán, a War of Independence hero, lived here in the early 1800s.

Casa del Inquisidor (14) The House of the Inquisitor at Cuadrante 18 was finished on June 6, 1780, according to a crude inscription on one of the beams in the house and on the front of the building. It was owned for a time by Victorino de las Fuentes, who is thought to have been an advisor to the Holy Inquisition. The building across the street on the corner of Hernández Macías is often referred to as the Inquisition's jail, although there is no evidence to support this. The last recorded activity of the Holy Inquisition in Mexico took place in Mexico City in 1817. On the northeast corner of Cuadrante and Hernández Macías is a beautiful *nicho* of a green cross, said to be a symbol of the Holy Inquisition.

Instituto Allende (15) The building known for more than half a century as the Instituto Allende was built, beginning in 1735, by Manuel Tómas de la Canal on a huge property on the *Salida a Apaseo*, (now Ancha de San Antonio), one of the main roads in and out of the city. The building was never a residence as has

often been written, but was a commercial enterprise consisting of workshops, storage areas, offices, and other industrial buildings. The property was surrounded by acres of orchards.

In 1809 nuns of a barefoot Carmelite Order from Querétaro, planning a new convent, bought the building, adjoining property, and orchards from the Canal family for 8,152 pesos. Ignacio Allende was a witness to the sales agreement. Great changes were planned with the help of the famous Spanish architect Manuel Tolsá, including the building of a church on the northeast corner of the property. The cost of turning the building into a convent would be covered by "a man who does not want his name to be known." Religious permits for the architectural changes were obtained in November, but the civil Royal Document that would confirm it never arrived. Ten months later in September 1810, the War of Independence began and the project was abandoned. The property eventually reverted to members of the Canal family. Over the years, the building was abandoned and vandalized. In the late 1940s the property was acquired by several investors and restored to become an art school, the Instituto Allende.

An enormous mural on the east wall of the patio, entitled "*Ignacio Allende y La Historia de México*," showcases the history of Mexico.

In 2005 the Instituto Allende was divided into two parts. The brothers who had inherited the enterprise divided the property. Instituto Allende Viajes y Servicios (Travel & Services) at Ancha de San Antonio 20, would concentrate on commercial activities: galleries, eateries, fairs, tours, wedding catering, etc. The other half, known as Instituto Allende Escuela Superior de Arte y Cultura at Ancha de San Antonio 22, would concentrate on academic activities and continue to offer courses in language, painting, weaving, sculpture, photography, and jewelry making.

Parroquia de San Antonio de Padua (16) Construction may have been started as early as the mid-1800s but the altar was not finished until 1879, its dome not completed until the 1960s, and the second bell tower not finished until the 1970s. The church, two blocks southwest of the Instituto Allende on a quiet and pleasant plaza, is still sometimes called " *San Antonio de la Casa Colorada.*" The name goes back to the time before the church was built, when services were held in a building painted red.

The church is much visited on Tuesdays by those who go to ask for the grace of matrimony. In 1978 the neighborhood of San Antonio, having grown enormously, was designated a parish. Its patron saint, San Antonio de Padua is honored around the saint's day, June 13, with the famous *locos* parade.

Los Mercados, the Markets (17) The *Mercado* San Juan de Dios, is a smaller and less crowded covered market than the Ignacio Ramírez Market. It was opened in 1992 and is located in the neighborhood that shares its name, a few blocks west of the Jardín. This market, like its competitor, sells fruits, vegetables, meats and other food stuffs, but also flowers, clothing, shoes, and miscellaneous items. There are a dozen food stands and having keys made is a cinch.

From the 1950s to the early 1990s, a *tianguis*, an outdoor market was held on Tuesdays on a few narrow streets in this neighborhood and thus came to be called by expats the Tuesday Market. But rampant population growth, complaints from residents, and traffic problems prompted the authorities to move the activities to a 12-acre plot on the outskirts of town. (See The *Tianguis*, page 145.) A ramshackle open air bazaar called Mercado San Miguel adjoins the San Juan de Dios market on its backside.

Another nearby market with many small stalls is located along the Cachinches arroyo on the Avenida Guadalupe, and collectively called *El Parián*. (Parián was the name of a famous 17th century market in Mexico City. The word means "Chinese Market" in Tagalog.) Some neighborhoods feature outdoor mini-markets, especially on Sunday mornings.

Templo de San Juan de Dios (**18**) The church on Calle San Rafael a few blocks north and west of the *Jardín*, was built in 1770 under the supervision of the priest Juan Manuel de Villegas with much of his own money. First named after San Rafael, the church was then at the very edge of town. The complex included a hospital, originally for infectious diseases, as plagues regularly swept the countryside. The stewardship of the buildings was eventually passed on to members of the Order of San Juan de Dios, called *Juanitos*, who renamed the church after their saint.

Behind the church a cemetery was built in 1782 by the San Miguel parish priest Joaquin Hidalgo y Costilla, the brother of Father Miguel Hidalgo. The *Panteón Antiguo*, once much larger (divided into several sections according to class), adjoins the property to the north. Recently rehabilitated, it is open to the public on November 2, the Day of the Dead.

In 1935 the hospital became San Miguel's general civil hospital and remained so until 1961, when a new facility was opened on Calle Reloj. The former hospital was then converted into a primary school, one of the largest in town. (A modern public hospital, built in 2006, is located on the edge of town on the way to Querétaro.)

Los Pocitos, an Orchid Garden (Not on the map) A narrow pedestrian bridge crosses the arroyo next to the house on Calle Santo Domingo 40 and leads to *Los Pocitos* (The Little Wells), an orchid garden begun by Stirling Dickinson, whose house was next to the property. Dickinson started his garden in the early 1940s and it became the largest private orchid collection in Mexico. He bequeathed the property to Cante, a private non-profit organization that maintains the collection.

The spacious garden is built among the ruins of one of the many tanneries that once brought much prosperity to San Miguel. There are four greenhouses for orchids requiring special protection and greater humidity, but a large number of plants are grown outdoors.

The collection now holds nearly 2,000 plants, constituting 230 species from many parts of the world, some very rare. Dickinson himself discovered several species which have been named after him, among them *epidendrum dickinsonianum* and *cypripedium dickinsonianum*. A small cactus garden has been built on the rear of the property. There are cozy areas to sit and read or contemplate the plants. Although there are always some orchids in bloom, the best time to see them is in winter and spring.

Los Pocitos is open all year, Tuesday through Saturday from 10-2. Special appointments can be made by calling the telephone number posted at the entrance. A small fee is charged.

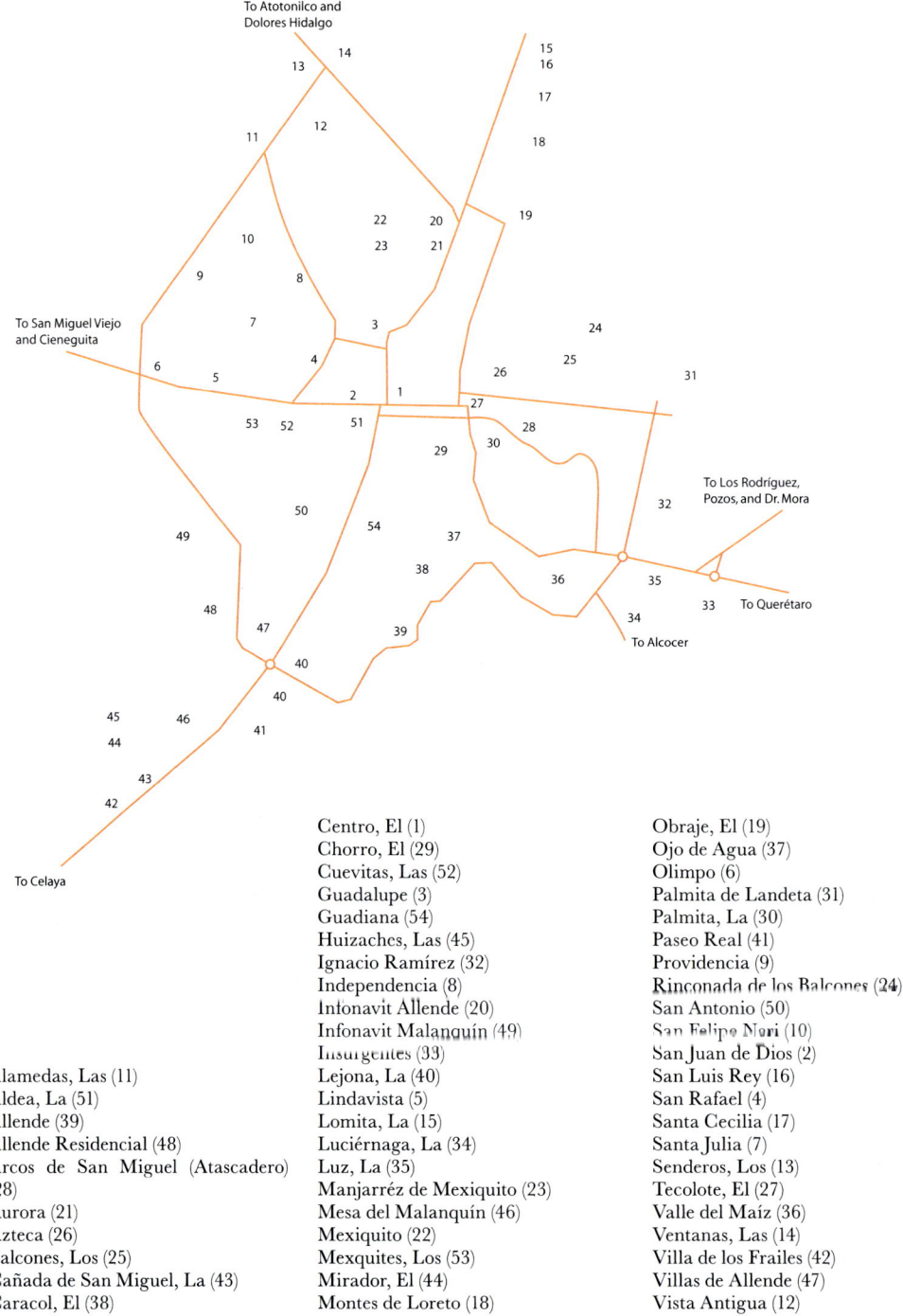

Alamedas, Las (11)
Aldea, La (51)
Allende (39)
Allende Residencial (48)
Arcos de San Miguel (Atascadero) (28)
Aurora (21)
Azteca (26)
Balcones, Los (25)
Cañada de San Miguel, La (43)
Caracol, El (38)

Centro, El (1)
Chorro, El (29)
Cuevitas, Las (52)
Guadalupe (3)
Guadiana (54)
Huizaches, Las (45)
Ignacio Ramírez (32)
Independencia (8)
Infonavit Allende (20)
Infonavit Malanquín (49)
Insurgentes (33)
Lejona, La (40)
Lindavista (5)
Lomita, La (15)
Luciérnaga, La (34)
Luz, La (35)
Manjarréz de Mexiquito (23)
Mesa del Malanquín (46)
Mexiquito (22)
Mexquites, Los (53)
Mirador, El (44)
Montes de Loreto (18)

Obraje, El (19)
Ojo de Agua (37)
Olimpo (6)
Palmita de Landeta (31)
Palmita, La (30)
Paseo Real (41)
Providencia (9)
Rinconada de los Balcones (24)
San Antonio (50)
San Felipe Neri (10)
San Juan de Dios (2)
San Luis Rey (16)
San Rafael (4)
Santa Cecilia (17)
Santa Julia (7)
Senderos, Los (13)
Tecolote, El (27)
Valle del Maíz (36)
Ventanas, Las (14)
Villa de los Frailes (42)
Villas de Allende (47)
Vista Antigua (12)

Barrios, Colonias, and *Fraccionamientos*

San Miguel de Allende counts more than 100 neighborhoods and developments, nearly all built in the last three or four decades.

The population of Mexico (and San Miguel) tripled during the last half of the 20th century, and the number of neighborhoods grew accordingly. The oldest areas nearest Centro, El Chorro, La Palmita, San Juan de Dios, Tecolote, Ojo de Agua, Valle del Maíz, and Las Cuevitas, are usually referred to as *barrios* (wards), while the *colonias* a bit further from the center of town are of more recent vintage: San Antonio, Guadalupe, Allende, Azteca, Guadiana, and others. If a *colonia* is particularly densely populated, the word *vecindad* (neighborhood) is sometimes used. *Fraccionamientos* are developments.

The map on the opposite page locates a number of neighborhoods in and around the city.

On Getting Around…

Walking is the preferred method of transportation and sturdy shoes are a must: the cobblestones are uneven; the sidewalks narrow, some streets are steep. But there are other ways to get around.

More than 100 buses, called *urbanos* or *camiones*, serving the city's many neighborhoods, are dispatched from two locations in the center of town. Buses leaving from Plazuela Zaragoza at the end of Calle Insurgentes go to neighborhoods and businesses such as San Antonio, Telmex, Telecable, Mega, the bus station, Los Frailes, La Aurora, or the immigration offices; buses headed for the *Tianguis* (Tuesday Market), Sapasma, City Hall, or the General Hospital are dispatched from the corner of Mesones and Colegio, at the Plaza Cívica. Nearly 50,000 people daily rely on bus transportation. The fares are kept low. Most buses run every 10 or 15 minutes. From Monday through Saturday they run from 6 a.m. to 9:30 p.m. On Sundays they run from 7 a.m. to 8 p.m.

Buses serving the outlying communities run only three or four times a day, and leave from various locations around the city, depending on the direction of the destination. Some leave from Puente de Umarán near the Ignacio Ramírez Market. Others leave from the San Juan de Dios Market, or from the Calzada de la Luz near Calle Loreto.

All the bus stops have dispatchers who can tell you about the bus's schedule. Buses are the greatest travel bargain in San Miguel. For around five pesos one can have a tour of most parts of the city. And for a few pesos more, buses can take the tourist to many of the outlying villages. If you are using the buses to see the rural sights, it is best to stay with your bus on arrival at your destination, unless you have a great deal of time. Keep in mind that the buses to the rural areas only arrive and depart a few times a day. The bus drivers have a real fondness for naming their vehicles.

There are more than 300 taxis registered in the municipality. Although the fees are set by state authorities, it is always a good idea to ask about the going rate. In San Miguel tipping is not expected by taxi drivers unless unusual services are performed. Rates usually go up about ten to twenty percent after dark.

The short blocks and narrow streets in the city keep traffic speed low, but once outside the city things speed up. While speed limits are posted, they are seldom enforced or adhered to. A half-century ago, the eminent historian Henry Bamford Parkes, in his "History of Mexico" already rued "the national fondness for driving as fast as possible." Still, in this town with no stop signs traffic is heavy but civil enough: drivers alternate on street corners and pedestrians, who have the legal right-of-way, are treated well.

Illegal parking is rampant. There are several kinds of police forces who patrol on foot, horseback, or vehicle. Instead of carrying guns, traffic cops carry a pair of pliers and a screwdriver in their holsters. An illegally parked car gets both a ticket attached to the windshield, and the license plate removed and taken to the police station, where it can be retrieved for a fee.

The wonderfully named *glorietas*, what the English call round-abouts and the Americans call traffic circles, are a fixture in many Mexican cities, since they are far cheaper to build than overpasses. There are several in San Miguel and they all have names: the *glorieta* at the end of the Salida a Celaya is called "*Pípila*" after the Independence War hero. The first glorieta east of the city is dedicated to General Ignacio Allende. He is shown on his horse, in full vigor, heading the liberation army in 1810. The last glorieta, the round-about of the Conspirators, is a mile further east, close to the new city hall. It displays statues of several of the Independence War Heroes (and one heroine): Allende, Hidalgo, Aldama, *La Corregidora* and St. Michael, slaying the devil.

Street Names

The first streets were named after saints or religious ideas, i.e., San Joaquín, La Purísima Concepción, San Antonio, etc. As the town grew, names that identified geographic or organic concepts were added: *Calle Molino de Abajo* (Lower Mill Street), *Callejón de las Higueras* (Alley of the Fig Trees), *Calle del Correo* (Post Office Street), and so on. Often sections of a street were simply named "Second block of … " or "Third block of … ," and so forth. After the War of Independence, and, a hundred years later, the Revolution, many street names were changed to honor political figures or war heroes. Calles Aldama, Umarán, and Corregidora are familiar examples.

Recent subdivisions and new suburbs tend to use themes: most of the streets in Colonia Guadalupe, for example, are named after composers, musicians, or even famous Mexican songs. Colonia Olimpo's streets are named after Greek gods and goddesses. In La Lejona, streets are named after natural phenomena: Echo, Lightning, Eclipse, etc. Extensions to streets were given new and different names, and so some streets change names every block. Chorro, for example, becomes Barranca, then Murillo, then Núñez, then Calzada de la Presa—five names for the same street within seven blocks. The confusion is compounded where some streets have received new names but the old signs are still embedded in the stucco walls of street corners. The visitor is further baffled by signs—left over from an earlier locating scheme—on nearly every street corner in the *Centro* reading "*Manzana*," with a number. Tourists find themselves on the corner of *Manzana* and *Manzana* and it doesn't help to know that "*manzana*" means both "apple" and "block."

Calle means "street," and a *callejón* is an alley. A *calzada* is a paved highway. *Andador* means "walkway," while *libramiento* means "freeway." Traffic circles are gloriously called "*glorietas.*" A *cuesta* is a hill or slope.

The tremendous growth of the population of Mexico in the last half-century added dozens of neighborhoods and nearly 1,000 streets to San Miguel, many with duplicate names. There are, for example, two streets called Guadalupe, three called Soledad, and four called San Juan (yet, only one is called Juárez, Mexico's most popular street name. There are more than 800 streets named "Benito Juárez" in and around Mexico City.) Of course, in San Miguel, the name Allende occurs with some frequency: There's an Avenida Allende, a Plaza Allende, a Calle Allende, a Privada Allende, even a *Cuna* ("cradle") de Allende.

Most of the names have been changed at one time or another. Streets named after saints or religious themes have seen the most changes and as recently as the first decade of the 21st century several street names were changed: Baeza, the street around part of Parque Juárez, named after an important family centuries ago was changed to Fray José Guadalupe Mojica, and the beltway, the *Libramiento*, was renamed Manuel Zavala Zavala in memory of a much-loved local radio personality.

Most street names have changed over the years, often reflecting major political or religious changes. For example, Nuñez was known for a time as *Los Diez Mandamientos* (The Ten Commandments). Insurgentes was first called *Los Trasteros*, then Santa Ana, and several blocks of Umarán were called *Cerritos* (Little Hills). San Antonio was renamed San Francisco and moved a block away; it was eventually renamed "Juárez." Zacateros was once called Santo Domingo, while Santo Domingo used to be called Calle del Atascadero. Cuadrante became the new name of Calle San Pedro y San Pablo. La Santísima Trinidad became known as Calle del Conde de Canal.

The signage, though, is rife with misspellings and other errors. The block once named after Venustiano Carranza still has a sign that says "E. Carranza." "*Huertas*" is misspelled as "Hurtas." Proper Spanish accents are often missing, and sometimes inappropriate abbreviations make life difficult for non-Spanish speakers: Hdez (for Hernández); Hnos (for Hermanos); and so on.

Listed below are the names of some streets, alleys, and plazas in and around the historic district, what their names signify, and how the names may have changed through the years. Many of the names, of course, can be found and their meaning deciphered, in dictionaries.

Alameda: Tree-lined walk or poplar grove.

Aldama: First called "*Calle del Hospital*" because of its proximity to a small 17th century hospital for Indians behind the *Parroquia*, it was renamed *Hermanos Aldama* (Brothers Aldama). (See Notables, page 125.) The third block was once called *Las Ánimas*, the fourth block Guadiana.

Ancha de San Antonio (broad or wide of St. Anthony) was originally named *Salida a Apaseo*, after the once important town 30 miles south of San Miguel.

Andador Lucas Balderas: *Andador* means "walkway." Lucas Balderas, born in San Miguel in 1797, was a war hero who died in battle in 1847, fighting the American invaders.

Aparicio: A family name.

Arboles: Trees.

Atascadero: Obstruction or mudhole. There are two streets named Atascadero, not very far apart. The name also refers to the subdivision above the city officially known as Arcos de San Miguel.

Baeza: Named after an important family for a hundred years, but changed in 2007 to Fray José Guadalupe Mojica.

Bajada del Chorro: The slope of the spurt. In the early 1800s, after baths were built next to the spring, the street was for a time called *De los Baños* (Of the Baths).

Barranca: Gully or gorge. The southern-most block was once named *El Chorillo* (The Little Spout or Spurt), after *El Chorro*, the nearby spring. The second block was named *Reboceros* (Rebozo-makers) for many years.

Bayoneta: Known in the 19th century as *Callejón de la Huerta Grande* (The Alley of the Big Orchard).

Callejón San Antonio: Once known as *Callejón San Benito*.

Callejón de los Muertos: Alley of the Dead. The one-block long alley leads from Calle Quebrada to the old municipal cemetery. Its former name was *Callejón de Sepultureros* (Alley of the Gravediggers).

Calvario: Calvary, Golgotha, the hill on which Jesus was crucified. The alley was known for years as *Callejón del Atascadero*.

Calzada de la Presa: Roadway to the Dam.

Cañadita de los Aguacates: Little Glen of the Avacados.

Canal: Named after members of the Canal family (see Notables, page 130). The street was originally called *La Santísima Trinidad* (The Holy Trinity), and then *Calle de la Purísima Concepción*, after the church and convent of that name were built on one of its blocks. Sometimes written as "*Conde de la Canal.*"

Cardo: Thistle. Once called *Cerrito de los Cardones*, the Little Hill of the Thistles. Also called *Calzada del Cardo*.

Chiquitos: Little Ones, probably referring to the many small houses on this narrow street. Originally called *Calle de los Domínguez* (a family name), it was also sometimes called "*Chiquitas.*"

Chorro: Spurt, or stream. It refers to the spring that served the community for more than 400 years.

Codo: Elbow. An appropriate name for a street with an abrupt turn. There are two streets named Codo.

Corregidora: Female Magistrate. It was originally and aptly called *Calle Corta* (Short Street).

Correo: Post Office. Before the post office was opened in the late 1700s, the street was known as *Calle de Nuestra Señora de Guadalupe* (Street of Our Lady of Guadalupe).

Cuadrante: Dial or Quadrant. It was originally called *Calle San Pedro y San Pablo*.

Cuna de Allende: Cradle of Allende.

Diez de Sollano: First Creole bishop in Mexico. Originally called *Calle San Juan Evangelista*, the name was later changed to *Calle del Conde* after the Count of Loja, a prominent San Miguel citizen, whose mansion occupied most of the first block of the street.

Diezmo Viejo: Old Tithe. The origin is unknown. Tithing (giving one-tenth of one's agricultural earnings to the Church) was the law in Mexico until after Independence.

Fray José Guadalupe Mojica: The famous singer and actor turned friar, then priest.

Garita: Sentry box. A family name.

Garza: Heron. A family name.

Guadiana: River of Ducks. The etymology of "*Wadi Ana*" is part Arabic and part Latin, "*Wadi*" meaning "river" in Arabic and "*Ana*" meaning "ducks" in Latin. The 778 km (483 miles)- long Guadiana River forms part of the border between Spain and Portugal. The street has also been known as *Callejón de las Quemadas* (The Alley of the Fires) and as *Calle de Correa* (Alley of the Belt or Strap).

Dr. Hernández Macías: A much-loved physician and mayor of San Miguel in the first decade of the 20th century. Its four blocks have variously been known as *Callejón de las Higueras* (Alley of the Fig Trees); *Calle de Volcán* (Street of the Volcano); *Calle de las Hojas* (Street of Leaves); *Calle de la Maestranza* (Street of the Arsenal).

Hidalgo: Father Miguel Hidalgo y Costilla (see Notables, page 134). First named *Calle de la Aduana*, (Street of the Customs Office). Several other blocks were named *de las Crucitas* (of the Little Crosses).

Homobono: A family name.

Hospicio: "Poorhouse," "hospice," or "asylum." In the 1600s an Indian hospice was located behind the *Parroquia*. By 1683 it was already reported to be "crumbling."

Huertas: Market gardens, or orchards.

Indio Triste: Sad Indian. Its origin is unknown.

Insurgentes: Once called San Felipe Neri, it was originally called *Calle de los Trasteros* (Dish makers) but later renamed *Avenida Santa Ana*, after the church of the same name next to the *Biblioteca Pública*, then renamed after Independence to honor the insurgents.

Juárez: Named for Benito Pablo Juárez García, who served five terms as president of Mexico, holding office from 1858-1872. The street was first called San Francisco.

Ladrillera: Brickyard.

Mesones: Inns. First known as Calle San José, five-block long Mesones was named eventually for the many inns that lined the street and provided food, lodging, and stables for the stream of merchants, travelers, and mule drivers who passed through San Miguel el Grande, beginning in the second half of the 16th century.

Montes de Oca: A family name, possibly after the first governor of the State of Guanajuato.

Montitlán: A somewhat awkward translation from Náhuatl would be "A Place in the Country."

Murillo: A family name.

Nueva: New. It became a "new" street when the *Regadera* arroyo was covered in the mid-1980s. The street has also been called *Paseo del Parque*. In 2009 the street was renamed Nemesio Diez, after a prominent businessman.

Núñez: A family name. The street was once called "*Los Diez Mandamientos*" (The Ten Commandments).

Órganos: Organ cacti.

Orizaba: The snow-covered 18,700-ft Pico de Orizaba, Mexico's highest mountain, 170 miles east of Mexico City.

Pedro Vargas: In 1978 several blocks of the Salida a Querétaro were renamed after the famous singer.

Pepe Llanos: The one-block-long street was named after a San Miguel-born hero of the Revolutionary War.

Piedras Chinas: Pebbles, cobblestones.

Pila Seca: Dry fountain.

Pilancón: Stone trough. The old drinking trough is still in place (although now used as a flower planter) on the corner of the alley and Calle Beneficencia.

Plaza Cívica: First known, in the latter part of the 16th century as *Plaza de la Soledad*, it was until 1737 the original town plaza. The smaller, western part of the plaza was named "*Plaza de Nuestra Señora de la Salud*."

Plaza Garibaldi: The plaza at the western end of Calle Organos is named after Giuseppe Garibaldi, the Italian patriot and general who was much-admired in Mexico.

Plazuela Zaragoza: General Ignacio Zaragoza and his troops defeated a French army, in the Battle of Puebla, on May 5, 1862.

Plazuela San Felipe: Named after San Felipe Neri.

Portal de Allende: The covered corridor on the west side of the Jardín, named after Ignacio Allende.

Portal de Guadalupe: The covered corridor on the east side of the Jardín was once called Portal de Lanzagorta, after the owner of the mansion on the southeast corner.

Potranca: Filly, young mare.

Potrero: Grazing field for horses.

Quebrada: The word can mean "ravine" or "gorge," but also "broken." Until the bridge was built over Calle Canal (in 1950), the street was broken in two by the gorge.

Recreo: Street of Recreation (or Leisure) was once called *Calle del Molino de Abajo* (The Street of the Lower Mill).

Reloj: Clock Street, still sometimes written as *Calle Relox*, (the spelling of which was officially changed by the Spanish Royal Academy in the 1930s), so named because for much of its length the clock of the San Rafael (Santa Escuela) church is visible. The street was originally called San Joaquin.

Salida Real a Querétaro: "Royal Exit to Querétaro." The first block was once called *Calle del Calvario*, after the chapel on top of the hill, while the second and third block were once named Santo Domingo, after the Dominican church on the corner. In 1978 several blocks of the street were renamed Pedro Vargas (see Notables, page 139).

San Dimas: "The Good Thief" who was crucified alongside Jesus.

San Francisco: The street was first named San Antonio, after the first convent. When Franciscan friars took over the convent, the name was changed.

Santo Domingo: St. Dominic. Originally named *Arroyo del Atascadero*.

Suspiros: Alley of the Sighs. Once known as Santa Catarina, it was at some point also called *Callejón de la Trampa* (Alley of the Snare or Trick).

Tecolote: Owl

Tenerías: Tanneries. Many tanneries were located along this street, taking advantage of the water available in the nearby *Regadera* arroyo.

Terraplén: Embankment.

Umarán: Juan de Umarán was one of the heroes of the War of Independence. Until the 1950s the lowest of the street's seven blocks was called *Calle de las Ladrilleras* (Street of the Brickyards), while the long, steep section in the middle was called *Calle del Cerrito* (Street of the Little Hill). Several other blocks were once named San Miguel.

Vergel: Flower and fruit garden, place of abundance.

Zacateros: Shown on some early maps as Zacatecas, the word refers to harvesters of a certain type of grass. It was briefly called "*Calle del Capitán Lorenzo Rodríguez*," after a military hero who in 1857 successfully squashed a small, unofficial American invasion in Sonora.

Zavala Zavala, José Manuel: For decades he was the beloved voice of San Miguel's only radio station, XESQ-1280 AM. After his death, in 2006, the *libramiento*, the freeway around San Miguel, was named after him. A bronze bust is displayed in the first block of Calle Sollano, across the street from the radio station. His nickname was *PPKBZON*, which, when pronounced in Spanish, sounds like "*pepecabezón*" ("*pepe*" being short for José, and *cabezón* meaning "big-headed").

5 de Mayo: The Battle of Puebla, and the (temporary) defeat of the French on that date in 1862.

16 de Septiembre: The day the War of Independence began in 1810.

20 de Enero: January 20, once thought to be the birthday of Ignacio Allende, but now officially celebrated on January 21.

28 de Abril: The name may be related to 28 April, 1836, when Spain finally officially recognized Mexico's independence. Some residents insist it was the birthday of the first person to build a house on the street!

House Numbers

House numbers, of course, were not needed in the early years of the small settlement of San Miguel el Grande, but as the town grew in size, numbering of houses on the streets became necessary. In the 1930s the city came up with a scheme to make all the house numbers, at least in the Centro, consecutive and identical in look. A simple design was chosen, a small rectangular white tile with a blue number and a serrated blue edge, and every house eventually sported the same design. In the *Centro* most still do, but over the years many numbers were painted or stuccoed over, renovations were made, or a more individual design was chosen.

So house numbers in the historical center of town are generally sequential and predictable, but the numbering system even a few blocks from the *Jardín* tends to be chaotic, varied and confusing. In the last block of Umarán, for example, this consecutive sequence occurs on one side of the street: 9, 79, 81B, 95, 3B, 5, 51B, 107, 144, 75, 93, 79, 81, 71, 91, 73, 77, and 5. On the other side of the block these numbers appear: 98, 18, 20, 13, 122, 22, 10, 11, and 164. Another sample: the numbering on the first block of the Ancha de San Antonio begins 3, 1, 3B, 9, 13, 11A, 15A, 23, 25, 9, 11 … and ends with the numbers 75, 47, 79, 81, 8, and 53!

While in most places even and odd numbers are used on opposite sides of a street, that is not necessarily the case in San Miguel. Nor do the numbers start in a predictable direction. In many cities numbering begins at the point closest to the center of the city, or City Hall, but in San Miguel that system cannot be relied upon. The lowest numbers on Calle Mesones, for example, begin at the farthest point from the center of the city.

There may be identical numbers in the same block for different houses, and one house may have several numbers.

The actual numbers are executed in countless ways: tile is popular, but paint is cheap. Brass will last a long time, as will rebar. There are house numbers executed in wood, in cardboard, in bottle caps. Numbers have been cast in cantera, the local limestone, or in solid bronze. The house number at Calzada de la Presa 15 is in Braille.

The enormous population increase in Mexico in the last half-century spurred the unregulated building of hundreds of houses in many neighborhoods. (Zoning is not practiced and city planning is only a recent activity.) San Miguel de Allende now has nearly 100 named neighborhoods, and the numbering system on many streets remains chaotic.

More than Four Dozen Fountains

San Miguel de Allende boasts four dozen public fountains (called *fuentes* or *pilas*) and nearly every house has a fountain in its patio. Modern plumbing has made most of the fountains obsolete, but many still function, to the delight of tourists and townspeople alike. Fountains were originally possible because of the copious spring called El Chorro, located on a rise above the town. Since the 18th century water was distributed to the citizens through a well-organized network of both underground and above-ground clay pipes. Several pipes that ran from El Chorro and the springs at Ojo de Agua eventually intersected on a corner of the Jardín. Other pipes were directed toward the many orchards around the city. A manual distribution system using mesquite wood doors as gates were opened or closed according to a timetable established in every water concession contract. Any person was allowed to draw water from the public fountains, as were the *aguadores*, the water merchants who made home deliveries in large cans or pots, charging only for the delivery service.

Many of the fountains have names. Here are some two dozen of the most interesting, along with their location:

Fuente de la Merced (corner of Cuadrante and Aldama).
Fuente de la Concha (Jesús, near Cuadrante).
Fuente del Conde (Sollano, near Correo).
Fuente Izquinapan (in front of La Casa de la Cultura, El Chorro).

Fuente los Aldama (Ancha San Antonio 26, next to the Instituto Allende). The fountain was moved from the birthplace of the Aldama brothers on Calle San Francisco, when that building was turned into a movie theater in the 1960s.

Fuente de los Insurgentes (corner of Quebrada and Insurgentes).

Fuente de Ignacio Allende (corner of Zacateros and Pila Seca). The fountain was installed in 1848 at the Calle Canal and Quebrada intersection. When the bridge over Canal was built in 1950, the fountain was moved to its present location. The inscription reads "A la Memoria del Varón Illustre Primer Caudillo La Libertad, Ignacio Allende" (To the Memory of the Illustrious Leader of Liberty, Ignacio Allende).

Fuente de Chata (corner of Aldama and Cardo). One of the largest and oldest fountains in San Miguel, it is also known as Golpe de Vista. A sign notes that the fountain was renovated in 1850 and thus probably dates back to shortly after Independence, since it is dedicated to "16 de septiembre de 1810."

Fuente de los Escudos (Correo, corner of Chiquitos).

Fuente de los Dolores (Murillo, between Correo and San Francisco).

Fuente de Madero (corner of Mesones and Hernández Macías), dedicated to President Francisco Madero.

Fuente Escuadrón 201 (corner of Recreo and Hospicio). The fountain is dedicated to the Mexican Expeditionary Air Force. When Nazi Germany torpedoed Mexican oil tankers that supplied the United States, Mexico joined the Allies and sent a P-47 fighter squadron that took part in MacArthur's invasion of the Philippines in 1945. Escuadrón 201, called the "Aztec Eagles," flew 96 missions. Five pilots were killed. It was the only time that Mexican forces have fought in a foreign war. The unit consisted of about 300 airmen, including 33 pilots.

Fuente del Cardo (corner of Ancha San Antonio and Cardo). The inscription reads "For the very illustrious town council of this city of Allende, 1828." As late as the 1960s it was the only source of water for nearly 100 families in the neighborhood.

Fuente de la Barranca (corner of Hospicio and Barranca). Sometimes also called Fuente de la Sirena, after the (damaged) mermaid sculpture, it was installed near the end of the 18th century.

Fuente de los Milagros (corner of Codo and Tenerías).

Fuente del Palmar (corner of Reloj and Palmar).

Fountains without names are found in many places: On a small plaza between the Oratorio Church and the Templo de la Salud is the site of one of the oldest fountains in San Miguel, dating from 1613, when permission was granted to conduct water from the Chorro spring to this area, when it was the main plaza of San Miguel. The Biblioteca has a good-sized working fountain in the patio. There are four fountains in the Jardín, three in Parque Benito Juárez.

Every year on Viernes de Dolores (Friday of Sorrows), the Friday before Palm Sunday, many of the fountains are cleaned and lavishly decorated in the afternoon with traditional offerings by families that live near. Bitter oranges, signifying the Virgin's Tears, along with lilies, chamomile and other white flowers are displayed. Crepe paper in purple and gold colors dominates. The decorations are only displayed during the night and are removed early on Saturday morning.

A Hundred Bells and Other Sounds...

Nearly a hundred bells hang from the *campanarios* (bell towers) and *espadañas* (belfries) of the score of churches and chapels scattered throughout the city. Each is dedicated to a particular saint or religious idea.

La Parroquia de San Miguel Arcángel, the parish church, boasts nine bells. The highest in the tower, and the largest and loudest, *la campana mayor* (the big bell), named after San Miguel, is eight inches thick at the rim and almost six feet tall. It dates back to the 19th century. Four *esquilas* (bells that have wooden tops and are rung by being tumbled over and over by hand), hang at the front of the church. They are only rung every Sunday at 11:30 and 11:45 a.m. and at noon. Two regular bells hang on each side. All supposedly have names, but only three have those names inscribed around the rim: La Luz, the oldest, from 1732, and Señores San Miguel and San Pedro, from 1838. The other bells have various names, sometimes made up by the *campanero*. One of the bells is called "Candelaria," but nobody can remember which one it is. The big bell is rung three times every day, at noon, at 3 p.m. (to commemorate the death of Jesus), and around 8 p.m. (*La Bendición*, blessing the entire city). The smaller bells, used to announce Mass, can be rung with ropes from ground level, but the *campanero* has to make the ascent to the tower to ring the heavy big bell three times a day, more often during certain fiestas. And during fiestas all bets are off, and the bells are rung at indeterminate times. In the Parroquia, as many as a dozen youngsters may be involved in the continuing cacophony of a *repique*, a simultaneous ringing, "a heady delight for small boys given the task."

The Santo Domingo church, at the east end of Calle Correo, has five bells (it looks as if there are only four, but one is suspended in the *espadaña* on the north side of the church). Other old bells are hung in the San Antonio church, the chapel of San José, and of course the bells in the church with the clock, San Rafael (Santa Escuela). Bells traditionally have their date of casting stamped on the rim, but the faking of antique bells is a thriving cottage industry in Mexico.

It is difficult to explain much of the ringing. The call to Mass, of course, begins early in the morning, at different times in different churches. The bells are rung three times for each Mass, each time for about 30 or 40 peals. The first rings at 30 minutes before the start of the Mass, the second at 15 minutes, and the third bell indicates that the priest is at the altar. Bell ringing is performed for both religious events and national fiestas. Extra chimes may be allowed on the saint's feast day.

On the first Friday of each month, at noon, all the bells at the San Antonio church are rung for a few minutes announcing a religious rite.

The bells in the clock tower of San Rafael, the church next to La Parroquia, toll every quarter-hour. The method of telling time by the sound is a mystery to many people, but it is really quite easy: two different bells are sounded, one announcing the quarter-hour, and the other, deeper peal, the hour. Thus, at first there are two peals, "bing-bing": one set of two strikes at a quarter after the hour; two sets of two on the half-hour; three sets of two at a quarter to the hour, and four sets of two on the hour. Then, in each case, after a short interval a different sounding bell tolls the hour. For example, half past four sounds like "ding-ding, ding-ding, dong, dong, dong, dong."

But other sounds permeate the city: there is the clang made on a triangular metal tympani that announces the imminent arrival of the garbage truck. The (un-pasteurized) milk truck uses a melodic claxon. The knife sharpener (on a bicycle) offers a repetitious faintly Peruvian melody on a flute. The propane trucks have various ways to announce their presence, often with loud and annoying music. Peanut and corn sellers peddle their products at the top of their voice.

Rockets and other fireworks are exploded at all times of day (especially at dawn) and for any conceivable reason: a birth, a death, a wedding, a baptism, a birthday, a saint's day, a fiesta, and other, sometimes mysterious events.

A Miscellany of Doors and Door Knockers

Visitors always remark on the great variety of the doors in San Miguel, and it is true that the citizenry prides itself on the individuality and creative diversity of the few aspects of their homes that can be seen from the outside. The same can be said of the choice of door knockers and the use of niches on the façade of buildings.

Some Notables

Since its founding nearly 500 years ago, a number of personages, some well-known, others a bit obscure, have been associated with San Miguel de Allende. Here are mini-biographies of some of them:

Aldama, Juan and Ignacio Heroes of the War of Independence, the brothers Aldama, Juan José and Ignacio Antonio, were born in San Miguel el Grande—Juan, in 1774 and Ignacio, in 1765—in a house on San Francisco 6. (After the Independence uprising the Spanish crown confiscated the property, which was abandoned for years and essentially destroyed when converted in the 1960s to a movie theater and later to an office. Almost nothing remains of the original structure.)

The well-to-do Aldama family owned tanneries in León and San Miguel. Both brothers attended the Colegio de San Francisco de Sales in San Miguel while Ignacio later attended university in Mexico City and became a lawyer. He prospered running a large tannery in the Atascadero. Juan enlisted in the Queen's Dragoons Regiment and attained the rank of captain in 1809. Both brothers were involved in the independence conspiracy and served with distinction in the War. Juan was the messenger who carried the news of the discovery of the plot to Allende and Hidalgo in Dolores. Ignacio Aldama was elected mayor of San Miguel after the city was liberated and was later named an envoy to the United States. He was caught in San Antonio Bejár, (now San Antonio, Texas) after an attempt to enlist for the rebels from the U.S. government. His instructions and credentials confiscated, he was taken to Monclova where he was executed on June 20, 1811. Juan was caught along with Ignacio Allende and José Mariano Jiménez in northern Mexico and executed in Chihuahua on June 26, 1811.

Alfaro, Luis Felipe Neri de   Born in Mexico City in 1709, Luis de Alfaro came to San Miguel el Grande in 1730 after graduating from the university when he was only 20 years old. He was admitted to the Oratorio and ordained a priest five years later. Devoted to St. Felipe Neri, he began calling himself Luis Felipe Neri de Alfaro. He became friends with Manuel Tomás de la Canal, like himself a rich Creole (from Spanish parents, but born in New Spain) from Mexico City. He inherited a great deal of money from his parents. Between 1730 and 1740 he rebuilt San Rafael, the "old" parish church and turned it into a religious school. He also financed the construction of the church of Our Lady of Health, Nuestra Señora de la Salud. His inheritance also helped to rebuild the Calvario chapel. He began the construction of the Santuario de Jesús Nazareno at Atotonilco in 1740.

An ascetic, Alfaro regularly flagellated himself, wore a hair-shirt, and, it is said, often spent the night in a coffin with a skeleton. On Good Fridays he would carry a heavy wooden cross from Atotonilco to San Miguel, a tradition still maintained almost 300 years later.

Robert Somerlott wrote that "In terms of building and tradition, Father Alfaro is the man who left the greatest mark upon San Miguel. In the centuries since his death, there has been an intermittent movement toward his canonization, but so far with little result."

He died in 1776 and was buried in the sanctuary in Atotonilco.

Allende y Unzaga, Ignacio María José de Jesús Pedro Regalado de   The most notable, of course, is Ignacio de Allende. After all, a sign above the entrance to the house he was born in, on the corner of Cuna de Allende and Umarán reads in Latin "Hic natus ubique notus" (Born here, known everywhere). He was born on January 21, 1769, the fifth of six children of a wealthy Basque merchant named Don Domingo Narciso de Allende and Doña Mariana de Unzaga. (A plaque near the entrance to the museum lists January 20 as his birth date, but during the bicentennial celebration of his birth the date was changed and the official celebration now takes place on 21 January.). He was baptized on January 25, 1769 in the parish church of San Miguel across the street.

Little is known about his early years. Tradition has it that he was impetuous and restless and not much is known about his education. Although he may have attended the Colegio de San Francisco de Sales, there is no record of his graduating. There are allusions to an interest in bullfighting, horsemanship, gambling and amorous adventures. He has been described by one historian as "decisive, impulsive, courageous, and fond of gambling and women as well as all kinds of fun." A contemporary called him "elegant and handsome…tall, with blond and curly hair and beard; white-skinned; blue and very lively eyes…a well-shaped mouth, always bearing a suspicious smile that could show either condescendence or disdain. He was athletic and always showed it in all his gestures and movements."

He sired the first of several illegitimate children at age 23. (One son, Indalecio, was killed in 1811 in action at Acatita de Baján, in Northern Mexico; another, José Guadalupe, fought against the Americans during the 1847 invasion.) Their father joined the Queen's Dragoon Regiment in 1795, becoming a lieutenant in the Third Company by purchasing, as was the custom, the grade of lieutenant and advancing to captain in 1809. He served under several well-known generals in, among other places, San Luis Potosí and Jalapa, "where he proved his skill and military intuition.…" In 1802, at age 33, Allende married an heiress, María de la Luz Agustina de las Fuentes, in one of the chapels of the Santuario de Atotonilco. She died six months later.

After his regiment returned to San Miguel in 1808 Allende began participating in secret meetings with the goal of plotting the overthrow of the Spanish government. He became acquainted with Father Miguel Hidalgo, the parish priest of Dolores who also belonged to one of the most active groups (the Literary and Social Club of Querétaro). Captain Allende became one of its leaders. An uprising was planned to take place at the annual winter fair in San Juan de los Lagos in October. The Spaniards discovered the scheme, but the wife of the chief magistrate (corregidor) of Querétaro, Josefa Ortiz Domínguez, and forever after known as "La Corregidora," had a message smuggled to Allende warning him of the discovery of the plot. Allende in Dolores conferred with Father Miguel Hidalgo. They decided to launch the revolt without delay and the following morning, September 16, 1810, the struggle for Independence was enjoined. They set off with their rag-tag army of unarmed Indian peasants toward San Miguel. In San Miguel Captain Allende imprisoned the Spaniards, saved them from mob vengeance and persuaded the local regiment, his own Dragoons of the Queen, to remain in their quarters.

Several months later, after a rout of the insurgents, Allende, Hidalgo, and many other leaders fled northward toward the U.S. border, but were captured in March 1811. By this time Allende was the generalissimo. He was caught and tried in Chihuahua, where he died before a firing squad on June 26, 1811. His severed head, along with those of three other leaders (Miguel Hidalgo, Juan Aldama, and Mariano Jiménez), was hung in a cage from a corner of the Alhóndiga de Granaditas, the granary in Guanajuato, the scene of a massacre of the Spanish at the beginning of the insurrection. The four cages were not removed until Independence was achieved a decade later.

His body was first buried in the Chapel of the Third Order in Chihuahua. In 1824 the remains were reburied in the Cathedral in Mexico City, and eventually at the Monument to Independence on the Paseo de la Reforma in Mexico City.

On March 8, 1826, the Congress of the State of Guanajuato renamed San Miguel el Grande, San Miguel de Allende, after its native-born patriot.

Bustamante, Anastasio Twice president of Mexico, Anastasio Bustamante was born in 1780 in the state of Michoacán. He studied medicine and practiced in San Luis Potosí, but began a military career in the Army of New Spain at the beginning of the War of Independence in 1810, trying to suppress Allende and Hidalgo. A decade later, when independence had almost been achieved, Bustamante changed allegiance and became a devout supporter of Agustín Iturbide, soon to be the self-proclaimed Emperor Agustín I of Mexico. Bustamante, now a general, was able to add 6,000 men to Iturbide's army.

Bustamante was the person responsible for removing ("liberating," say some commentators) the heads, now skulls, of the four Independence War heroes: Allende, Hidalgo, Aldama, and Jiménez, from the cages on the four corners of the Alhóndiga de Granaditas in Guanajuato, although he himself had done his best, ten years earlier, to put them there. He became Mexico's Vice-President in 1828, then President in 1830. He was exiled in 1832 and went to Europe. He was recalled in 1837 and once again became President. The famed Fanny Calderón de la Barca met him and wrote, "He was once a doctor, and a very bad one he must have been. He reminds me of an old New York merchant, fat and pursey." He held office for four years, and then went  into exile again, this time to San Miguel de Allende, where he lived quietly at Calle San Francisco 38 until his death in 1853. Before burial his heart was removed, according to his wishes, and taken in a crystal flask to Mexico City where it was interred along with the remains of his great hero, Iturbide. He is buried in San Miguel in a corner of the crypt under the Parroquia de San Miguel Arcángel, a small Mexican flag partially covering the gravestone.

Cossío del Pomar, Felipe Born in 1888 in San Miguel de Piura, Peru, Cossío del Pomar, artist, art historian, and writer, who had first visited San Miguel in 1926 and had fallen in love with the then impoverished backwater town, returned to San Miguel in 1937 in hopes of starting a Latin American art school. He had been exiled from Peru for political reasons.

Tha same year, the president of Mexico, Lázaro Cárdenas, granted Cossío the use of a nearly ruined ex-convent on Calle Hernández Mácias, La Concepción (Las Monjas) that had for decades been used as barracks by an Army cavalry regiment. Cossío directed the renovations and named the school Escuela Universitária de Bellas Artes. The first students arrived in 1938. In 1945 it became possible for Cossío to return to Peru, but he was again exiled in 1948 and came back to San Miguel. In his absence the school was run with the help of Stirling Dickinson. The school was disbanded in 1949.

Cossío, who was wealthy, bought a number of properties in San Miguel. He acquired, for about 200 dollars, La Ermita, an abandoned rest stop for coaches on the Salida a Querétaro, and renovated it. He also purchased the bullring on Calle Recreo and had it fixed up in time for the 400th anniversary celebration in 1942 of the founding of San Miguel. After selling La Ermita, he bought the 200-acre Atascadero ranch on the Santo Domingo road from the famous bullfighter, Pepe Ortiz. In 1950, along with Enrique Fernández Martínez, he became one of the founders of the Instituto Allende. In 1952 Cossío bought and renovated El Retoño, also on the Salida a Querétaro, where he lived until the early 1970s. For a time he moved to Spain, where he published his "Cossío del Pomar en San Miguel de Allende," a recounting of his years spent in Mexico. In 1980 he was allowed once again to return to Peru where he died the following year at age 93.

Canal y Hervás, María Josefa Lina de la The oldest daughter of Manuel Francisco Tomás de la Canal y Bueno de Baeza, María Josefa was born on September 23, 1736. She "showed an inclination toward religion" and had "a soul filled with piety." At age 13, after the early death of both her parents, she expressed a desire to become a nun. She had inherited enough money to found and finance and, in 1755, to begin building a church and convent that came to be known as the Convento Real de la Immaculada Concepción, but which the people have always called Las Monjas (The Nuns). The building was not finished when at age 18 she joined the convent, then temporarily located in the San Rafael church (also known as "Santa Escuela"). She took her final vows at age 20 and became known as María Josefa Lina de la Santísima Trinidad.

A mystical person, she apparently had little interest in education or charitable work. "Her life," wrote her biographer, "consisted of fearing, desiring, admiring and loving Christ." She spent the last five years of her life in the not quite finished Concepción convent, where she died in 1770 at age 33, long before the final completion of the buildings. She had been a nun for 14 years. She was buried beneath the choir of the convent church she helped found.

Canal, Narciso María Loreto de la Born in 1758, Narciso was the son of José Mariano de la Canal and the grandson of Manuel Francisco Tomás de la Canal. Fearful of foreign invasions (Spain was at war in Europe), the viceroy offered inducements to members of the upper classes to join and support the militia. To men willing to contribute 40,000 pesos—the cost of equipping 350 men—he promised the position of commander-in-chief of their own local regiment. In 1795 Narciso and other well-to-do members of the San Miguel community offered to form and pay for a regiment to be called "Los Dragones de la Reina" (The Dragoons of the Queen). He contributed 24,225 pesos to the effort—more than half of the funds required, and thus became the commanding officer. His friend, Juan María de Lanzagorta, who contributed 5,648 pesos, became second in command. When the insurgents seized San Miguel on September 16, 1810, he kept his troops quartered. The writer Robert Somerlott questioned: "Was he secretly in cahoots with his friend and neighbor Allende? Or a coward? Or a commander sensible enough to avoid a massacre?" He went into hiding in Guanajuato after the rebel armies had left the city, but was arrested and imprisoned. Charged with "irresolution and…a strangely culpable omission," he was tried by a royal court in Querétaro. The prosecution lasted three years while Canal languished in prison, where he died in 1813. In the aftermath of the insurgency the Canal mansion, which Narciso had completed, was repeatedly vandalized by bandits and government forces.

Canal y Bueno de Baeza, Manuel Francisco Tomás de la Manuel Francisco Tomás de la Canal, born in 1701 in Mexico City of wealthy parents, was one of San Miguel's greatest benefactors. He moved to San Miguel in 1732 and married María Josefa de Hervás y Flores, the daughter of a wealthy mine-owner from Guanajuato, who brought a fortune of nearly a million pesos to the union. Manuel de la Canal donated money to charities, helped build roads and chapels and supported countless religious and civic projects, including the Oratorio church, the Colegio de Francisco de Sales, and the Santa Casa de Loreto. He owned several haciendas near San Miguel and an *obraje*, a textile mill. He built the *casa solariega* (now the Instituto Allende) in the early 1740s. The building was never used other than for commercial purposes, as office building, workshops and warehouses, and for storage. He and his wife both died in 1749, three days apart. They were buried in the Santa Casa de Loreto. The people of the town insisted that Don Manuel de la Canal "had fallen from heaven for the benefit of the Villa de San Miguel."

Dickinson, Stirling Born in Chicago in 1909, Dickinson first heard about San Miguel in 1935 while traveling in Mexico, when he met the famous Mexican actor and singer José Mojica, who mentioned that, as Dickinson later wrote, he "was stopping off at a little silver-mining town [sic], San Miguel Allende. He has heard it is even more beautiful than Taxco. We should go." Dickinson didn't for two years, but in 1937 he visited for the first time and he would stay in San Miguel until his death, 60 years later.

Shy, introverted, wealthy, a graduate of Princeton and the Art Institute of Chicago, he first traveled to Mexico in 1934 with a classmate, the writer Heath Bowman, to research the first of three books they eventually published, with Bowman as writer and Dickinson as illustrator. They arrived in San Miguel in 1937. The following year they bought the ruins of an old tannery on Calle Santo Domingo, which they called Los Pocitos (The Little Wells). They paid 90 dollars for the property. Bowman later married and Dickinson purchased his share of the house. He was to live there until his death. In 1938 Dickinson became the associate director of the first art school in

San Miguel, La Escuela Universitária de Bellas Artes. When the school closed in 1949, he opened his own, but a year later joined the Instituto Allende as its dean.

A philanthropist and active in the community, he helped with the construction of several schools, was a member of the board of the local hospital and Patronato Pro Niños, ran the Rural Schools Program of the Biblioteca Pública, and played for and managed the San Miguel baseball team which at one time won 86 consecutive games. He was an avid collector of orchids and a species he discovered in Chiapas was named after him: *encyclia dickinsoniana*. Another species, *cypripedium dickinsonianum*, was named after him in recognition of his botanical work (see Los Pocitos, an Orchid Garden, page 90). He was named "Favorite Adoptive Son of San Miguel de Allende" by the municipal authorities. He died in an automobile accident in 1998. A bust was installed on the Ancha de San Antonio on a corner across from a street named after him.

Díez de Sollano y Dávalos, José María de Jesús Born in 1820 on the first block of Calle Canal, José Díez de Sollano y Dávalos at age 12 was enrolled in the Colegio de San Francisco de Sales in San Miguel, where he studied until 1834, then completed his studies in Morelia and Mexico City and at age 22 taught at a seminary. Shortly after he was ordained a priest in 1844, he became dean of the Colegio de San Gregorio. He later taught at the University of Mexico. In 1863 he became the first Creole (Mexican-born Spaniard) cleric to be appointed bishop of the newly created Diocese of León, where he built more than 100 churches and the cathedral. He was described in chronicles of the time as a man "loaded with virtues." He authorized the construction of the new facade of the Parroquia in 1880. He died a year later. His statue stands on the tall obelisk in the atrium of the Parroquia.

Gutiérrez, Zeferino Born in San Miguel on August 24, 1840, and always described as a "humble, illiterate mason," Gutiérrez was in fact a highly skilled builder and architect who was responsible for building the new façade of the *Parroquia* 1880-1888, the tower and cupola of La Concepción and several other buildings in town. In 1876 he redesigned and rebuilt the Ermita chapel.

In 1896 he redesigned and reconstructed the clock tower of Santa Escuela. In 1901 he was responsible for the building of the Mercado Aldama, later known as the "flower market," now an open air restaurant. He built a number of buildings in Dolores Hidalgo. He has been associated with refurbishing the San Juan de Dios church and the Santo Domingo church. He has been much maligned by architectural critics, but the people of San Miguel and its many visitors adore his work, especially the façade of the Parroquia. Gutiérrez died on March 23, 1916 and is buried in a small side chapel of the San Rafael church next to the Parroquia.

Hidalgo y Costilla, Miguel "The Father of the Country" was born in 1753 near Pénjamo. A brilliant student and linguist, he studied at the Jesuit school in Valladolid (now Morelia) and was ordained a priest in 1778. By 1790 he had become rector of the college of San Nicolás. Soon after his appointment he was charged with reading prohibited books and with having a character "influenced by association with Jesuits, and scandalous relations with women." He questioned the virgin birth and the infallibility of the pope. (He had openly fathered two children in a relationship with Manuela Ramos Pichardo.) He lost his position as rector in 1792 and for the next ten years served as a parish priest. In 1802 he was reassigned to the small parish of Dolores. (In 1803 he traveled to San Miguel to officiate at the burial of his brother, Joaquin, who was the parish priest.)

Hidalgo read French, Latin, and Italian. He enjoyed music, played the violin, and held musical soirees in his home. He continued his illegal activities of making wine and raising silkworms and drew attention from the Holy Office of the Inquisition. It was charged that he was "free in his treatment of women" and that "in the house of this Hidalgo there has been enough riotous celebration to turn it into a little France. ..." He was censored but not prosecuted.

He became part of the independence conspiracy and proclaimed the famous "Grito," the Cry of Independence, on the morning of September 16, 1810. On the march to San Miguel he stopped at the Santuario de Atotonilco and took the banner of the Virgin of Guadalupe, naming her the patroness of the revolt. It was Hidalgo's indecisiveness and lack of military skill that doomed the early stage of the revolt. He fled toward Texas, was captured, tried, excommunicated, and executed in Chihuahua, on July 30, 1811.

Juan de San Miguel The Franciscan friar Juan de San Miguel (St. Michael, an archangel, was his patron saint) was born in Spain early in the 16th century, but the exact year or place is not known. It is thought that he came to Mexico around 1528, shortly after the Conquest. By 1531 he was working as a missionary in Michoacán where he helped found the College of San Miguel in Valladolid (now Morelia). In the late 1530s he worked in Uruapan, where he taught the Indians new methods of agriculture and instructed them in various arts and crafts.

In 1540 Fray Juan left Uruapan to become abbot at the Santa María de Gracia monastery in Acámbaro, 60 miles south of San Miguel. In the early 1540s he left the monastery to make his way north to evangelize the Indians at the present site of San Miguel and started a mission that came to be called "San Miguel de las Chichimecas." "His words," wrote one chronicler, "converted as many souls as there are pine trees in the mountains." After a short time, he left the mission in charge of another friar, and went on to evangelize other areas north of San Miguel. Sickly, in the spring of 1555 he returned to Uruapan, where he died on May 3, 1555, and was buried in the parish church.

The historian Francisco de la Maza wrote in 1939 that the founder of San Miguel was unjustly forgotten. He complained that no street, plaza, or monument was named after him, but prophesied that in 1942, at the forthcoming 400th anniversary of the founding that situation would be remedied. A bronze statue of the friar consoling an Indian was installed on the northwest corner of the Parroquia's atrium. In 2007 a small statue was unveiled at the chapel in San Miguel Viejo, the site of the original mission. There are now two streets in San Miguel named Fray Juan de San Miguel, not a great distance apart.

Martínez Amaro, Juan José de los Reyes "El Pípila" The name "Pípila" is famous throughout Mexico. It was the nickname of one of the heroes of the War of Independence. "Pípila" is a hen turkey and the name probably referred to the speckled coloration of a turkey's eggs, which may have been a cruel allusion to pockmarked skin. He was born, on January 3, 1782, in a modest house at Calle Barranca 44. He probably worked in the silver mines of Guanajuato before the War.

On September 28, 1810, shortly after the start of the War of Independence and after "liberating" Dolores, San Miguel el Grande, and Celaya, the insurgents descended on Guanajuato, where the Spaniards had barricaded themselves in the Alhóndiga de las Granaditas, a massive stone granary. The insurgents attacked, experienced heavy losses, but were unable to advance. Pípila took a large paving stone on his back to shield his body from bullets from above, and with a lighted torch in his hand advanced on one of the huge doors of the granary and managed to set it on fire. (Some accounts suggest that he may have used dynamite.) Once the opening was breached, the mob was able to enter. A horrible massacre ensued. Lucas Alamán described it in his "Historia de México"

> *When the insurgents had taken the Alhóndiga they gave rein to their vengeance. In vain, those who surrendered begged on their knees for mercy. ... Most of the soldiers of the battalion were killed, others escaped by taking off their uniforms and mixing with the crowd. ...*

It was one of the great tragedies of Hidalgo's leadership. Little is known of Pípila's life afterwards. He died on July 25, 1863, at age 81 "from colic and an acute pain."

An enormous monument high above Guanajuato was erected late in the last century. Each year on September 28 a civic ceremony is held in front of the house on Calle Barranca to pay homage to this humble man for his noble contribution to Mexico's independence. And every year on his birthday, January 3, a small wreath of flowers is placed in front of the house. In the late 1990s a statue of the hero was placed and dedicated in the middle of the Glorieta de Pípila, the traffic circle on the edge of town on the road to Celaya.

Mojica, José Francisco Guadalupe Born in Jalisco in 1895, Mojica became a famous singer and actor who performed in many films and opera houses in Mexico and the United States. He discovered San Miguel de Allende in the mid-1930s and spent 2,000 pesos for a ruin, the remains of a 15-acre hacienda on the edge of Parque Juárez that had originally been built in the late 1700s by the Count of Baeza. Mojica restored the property and frequently entertained famous actors, artists, poets, and writers, before entering the religious life in 1942. He joined the Third Order of the Franciscans, becoming a monk, and three years later was ordained a priest. He spent much of the rest of his life in a monastery in Lima, Peru. The building was sold in 1969 and became the Hotel Villa Santa Mónica. From time to time Mojica returned to the stage and screen (and wrote several books) in order to raise money for his Order and other charities, among them the Mexiquito Boys Orphanage on the outskirts of San Miguel. He died in Peru, in 1974. The street adjoining Parque Benito Juárez near the Villa Santa Mónica was renamed after him in 2007.

Ortiz de Domínguez, Josefa "La Corregidora" Josefa Ortiz de Domínguez, who lived from 1768 to 1829, was the wife of Miguel Domínguez, Querétaro's corregidor (mayor-magistrate). Beginning around 1809, with turmoil in Spain and the very legality of the viceregal government in New Spain in question, the plotters of the Independence Movement, who included Allende

and Hidalgo, would sometimes meet with Doña Josefa. They were discussing literary matters, she would explain to her husband. The insurrection was to take place in December, but the plot was discovered. On September 15, 1810, she sent a message through her husband's secretary, Ignacio Pérez, to her co-conspirators in San Miguel. She was arrested, found guilty, and kept in seclusion in several monasteries. In 1817 she was released upon swearing an oath that she would not support the rebels. One of Mexico's few acknowledged heroines, she came to be known as La Corregidora.

Peralta, Ángela An operatic soprano of international fame, Ángela Peralta was born in Mexico City on July 6, 1845. She made her debut in 1860 at age 15 at the National Theater, singing the role of Leonore in Verdi's "Il Trovatore." Performing in Europe in 1862 she sang at the famous La Scala opera house in Milan in a performance of "Lucia di Lammermoor." She became known as "El Ruiseñor Mexicano," (The Mexican Nightingale) and performed in Europe for many years. An artist of great versatility, she sang, acted, played the harp and piano with skill, and composed music.

She returned to Mexico in 1865 and divided the rest of her career between Europe and Mexico until 1871, when she formed her own opera company. In 1873 the operatic soprano, who had been performing in Guanajuato, was persuaded to come to San Miguel to inaugurate a new theater. Such was the excitement about her coming to San Miguel that when her carriage arrived at the outskirts of the city, "the crowd unhooked the mules from her carriage and pulled her themselves."

The first performance took place on Sunday, May 11, 1873 with Verdi's "Rigoletto," before an audience that not only filled the theater but the streets as well. She stayed in the city for more than a week to sing "Roy Blas," "Il Trovatore," and on her last day "Lucia di Lammermoor." The new theater was promptly named "Ángela Peralta."

Peralta returned to San Miguel once more in 1881 and sang "The Barber of Seville," and several other operas. She died in 1883 while performing in Mazatlán, then in the midst of a yellow fever epidemic. She was 38.

Ramírez Calzada "El Nigromante," Ignacio One of the most famous of San Miguel's native sons was Ignacio Ramírez, a controversial intellectual, writer, poet, essayist, philosopher, and politician, who wrote under the pen name "*El Nigromante*" (The Sorcerer). He was born on June 22, 1818, in a comfortable middle-class home at Calle Umarán 28. His father was at one time the vice-governor of the state of Querétaro. Ignacio Ramírez was educated in the city of Querétaro and received his law degree in Mexico City. He became a journalist and founded several liberal publications and newspapers. He also taught law and literature in Toluca. He wrote plays, articles and satirical poems which criticized the government. He was imprisoned for a short time in 1845, and again in 1852 during the Santa Ana regime.

"El Nigromante" was also a congressman, and became Minister of Justice during the Benito Juárez administration where he handled the nationalization of church property. During the reign of the Emperor Maximilian he was again briefly exiled, but returned to serve on the Supreme Court of Justice. He died suddenly on June 15, 1879.

When the Centro Cultural Bellas Artes was opened in 1962 it seemed appropriate to add the name "El Nigromante" to the new art school since he was born only a block away. Every year on his birthday school children from San Miguel parade past his house on Umarán, a touching tribute to a prolific liberal thinker and writer who represented the purest ideas of Juárez's Reforma.

Vargas, Pedro Pedro Vargas was born on April 29, 1906, in a house at Mesones 14. One of San Miguel's most famous sons and one of the most revered singers and proponents of Mexican music in the 20th century, he moved to Mexico City at age 14 where he met important composers and began singing professionally. He originally sang opera, but gained fame with his renditions of popular songs. Pedro Vargas could sing for three hours without stopping and it is said that he had a repertoire of more than 500 songs.

He built a large house on the Salida Real a Querétaro overlooking the city. A large bust of the singer sits next to the house, adjoining the Mirador. The name of the street was officially changed to Pedro Vargas in 1978, and is so named on many maps, but the locals still call the street "Salida."

He was also a pioneer in Mexico's recording and television industry in the 1950s and had a five decades long career and appeared in dozens of motion pictures. He was known as *"El Tenor de las Américas"* and *"El Samurai de la Canción"* (The Samurai of Song). He died in 1989. On the 100th anniversary of his birth, in 2006, a commemorative Mass was celebrated in San Miguel, attended by many famous Mexican entertainment personalities.

Interesting Places a Little Farther Away

El Tianguis, the Tuesday Market

On Tuesdays, there is a 12-acre outdoor market on the outskirts of town near the shopping center on the road to Querétaro. Called the *tianguis*, the Náhuatl word for market, it is usually referred to as the "Tuesday Market" by foreign residents and visitors. Nearly 1,000 merchants participate, but the entire enterprise is run as an incorporated business, with individuals paying rental fees for their stalls to the organization, which in turn pays the municipality. It is one of the largest outdoor markets in the state of Guanajuato. More than 10,000 customers visit each Tuesday (on other days many of the merchants show their wares in markets in Celaya, Dolores Hidalgo, and other towns).

The stands, varying in size from 10 to 30 feet, most covered by colorful plastic tarpaulins, offer an amazing variety of goods. Whether it is fresh fish, cell phones, strawberries, used bicycle parts, T-shirts, furniture, music CDs, or "seconds" in designer clothes, almost anything can be found except fireworks, weapons, alcohol, dogs, or prescription drugs. There are dozens of food stands offering all the usual Mexican dishes. And bartering, although not as common as before, still goes on with some of the vendors. It is a noisy, colorful, and crowded scene. Many tourists mistakenly believe that they should be in the market at the crack of dawn. In fact, although a few merchants start setting up at dawn, most are not ready for business until about nine o'clock. Mid-morning is really the best time, since the food is still fresh,  and the vendors are feeling friendly and energetic. By 5 o'clock in winter, later in summer, packing up and cleaning up begins. By dark not a trace of the activity of the day remains.

The Botanical Garden, El Charco del Ingenio

One of San Miguel's treasures is the 250-acre nature preserve and botanical garden, *El Charco del Ingenio* (The Millpond), so named since a mill was built there as early as the 1560s. El Charco was created in 1990 to preserve land on the outskirts of San Miguel. The preserve surrounds a canyon and reservoir about a mile above the city. A network of well-maintained and secure trails allows walks of 1.5 to 2 hours along the various sites of the preserve. It is a birder's paradise. Of the more than 1,000 species of birds found in Mexico, 156 species have been observed in El Charco del Ingenio. More than 500 species of flora and cacti, 19 species of reptiles, 16 species of mammals, and 9 species of amphibians have been counted and more than 100 species of butterflies have been sighted.

There are ruins of a hacienda across the dam of the presa, and in the rainy season there are ponds and waterfalls galore. A 1580 map shows a *molino de agua*, a water mill, on the edge of what is now a reservoir called Presa del Obraje. A map from 1723 shows two water mills and what appears to be a small canal, or ditch, between the mills and some springs.

Still in evidence, a huge iron pipe in the early part of the 20th century conveyed water from the reservoir to the La Aurora textile mill in order to generate electricity.

A Conservatory of Mexican Plants exhibits a botanical collection, with many outstanding species of cacti and succulents. Mexico has the richest variety of cacti in the world. The botanical collection is made up of plants gathered from all parts of the country along with others propagated in the nursery.

El Charco del Ingenio also functions as a recreational and ceremonial space for the community. In 1994 the local government ceded 35 hectares (about 85 acres) of adjacent land for a public park, Parque Landeta, where camping, picnics, horseback riding and mountain biking are allowed. The City also maintains its own nursery in the park. A small entry fee is charged.

The Botanical Garden is open daily from sunrise until sunset. The Conservatory is open from 9 a.m-4 p.m. A small fee is charged, but annual memberships, which allow for unlimited access, are available. Although the Botanical Garden is not more than a mile from the center of town, it's an uphill trek. Many visitors take a taxi up and walk back down.

The organization also owns a 222-acre oak forest preserve in the Picachos Mountains just south of San Miguel. Called "La Cañada de los Pajaritos" it is a 3- to 4-hour hike to the 8,500 feet high site.

Six Succulents

The Cactus family, *Cactaceae*, is native only to the New World and its plants extend from Canada to the tip of South America, with about 900 species in Mexico. These succulents have been used by humans for food, drink, medicine, building materials and ornamentals, and for ritual use. Cacti are a conspicuous feature of the vegetation around San Miguel, as are maguey and yucca, members of the *Agavaceae* family.

Maguey, known as Century plant or agave (from the Greek for "marvelous"), is not a cactus but a succulent. The flowering stem can grow to more than 20 feet. There are more than 400 species of maguey, and certain ones (*Agave americana* and *Agave salmiana*) provide the raw materials for mescal and tequila.

Yucca, also known as Joshua tree, is also a succulent. It can grow to more than 40 feet. The flower buds are edible, and the strong leaf fibers have been used for making rope. Several examples can be seen on the Prolongación de Santo Domingo near the Hotel Atascadero.

Cholla, also called *cardón*, is a contorted bush-like plant that grows from 3-10 feet. Reddish or purple flowers grow from the ends of branches. The inch-long fruit is yellow. The plant has been used for many purposes, as food and medicine (for stiff joints and bruises).

Nopal (Prickly pear) has stems of flat, rounded pads and can grow to 13 feet. The flowers are yellow, while the fruits are red. The fruit, 3-4 inches long, is called "*tuna*." The pads can be eaten after the spines are removed.

Órgano (Organ cactus) grows to a height of 10-18 feet, but occasionally to 40 feet and is often used as a living fence to keep livestock contained. The flowers are reputed to have been used to dye hair black.

Garambullo (Old Man cactus or Mexican blueberry) grows much like a tree and can reach to 30 feet high and 25 feet wide. This cactus is only found in Mexico. In pre-Hispanic Mexico the delicious purple fruit was an important food source.

150

The Chapel at San Miguel Viejo

San Miguel Viejo (Old San Miguel) is a small hamlet a mile west of the railroad station with a population of about 300 people. It was the original site of the mission begun by Fray Juan de San Miguel in the early 1540s. In 1551 the settlement was attacked and destroyed by marauding Indians. Nothing remains of any original structures. The mission was moved up the slope of the Hill of Montezuma to the spring at El Chorro and the present site of San Miguel.

The pretty chapel, set amid cornfields a few hundred yards outside the village probably dates from the mid-1700s. Tiny, with a walled-in atrium, it is typical of the thousands of Indian chapels that were built in Mexico. According to the historian Donna Pierce, "This building type evolved in response to several conditions: the Mexican Indians were accustomed to outdoor religious services; an immense number of Indian converts had to be accommodated…and large churches could not be constructed rapidly." Cost, of course, was always also a factor. Several *calvarios* (miniature shrines that allow offerings to be made) are scattered around the site, while pre-Hispanic religious symbols abound on the façade. A small statue of Fray Juan was installed in the atrium in 2006. The saint's day of San Miguel Arcángel is celebrated on September 29. Other festivities take place during the year, among them the celebration known as El Señor de la Conquista on the Sunday after the first Friday in March. Mass is celebrated in late afternoon on Mondays by the priest of the Parroquia de San Antonio de Padua.

The *Presas*... Reservoirs

The word "*presa*" can mean "dam" in Spanish, but the term usually refers to an actual body of water, a reservoir.

There are several presas near San Miguel, but the largest by far is the Presa Ignacio Allende, a reservoir constructed between 1964 and 1969 as a flood control measure at a canyon called La Begoña, on the Río Laja about eight miles southwest of the city. During the rainy season the Río Laja sometimes caused extensive flooding in the lower areas of the Bajío around Comonfort, Celaya, Salamanca, and Irapuato. The Presa was officially inaugurated on January 21, 1969, the bicentennial of Ignacio Allende's birthday. (The dam also made it possible, year-round, to cross the river and drive to Guanajuato without going through Celaya or Dolores.) With a 125-foot high steel and concrete dam it created a "twisted, contorted octopus of a lake," the largest body of water in this part of Mexico. About 12,000 acres (18 square miles) were inundated. (In the dry season, and in time of drought, the Presa is, of course, considerably smaller.) The enormous, curious 20-foot tall letters "S.R.H." on the downstream side of the dam stand for Secretaria de Recursos Hidráulicos (Office of Hydraulic Resources).

Many of the *campesinos* refused to believe that the usually sluggish Río Laja would inundate settlements for miles around and continued planting crops that were soon covered by the water along with many buildings, some settlements, a small hacienda, and some pre-Hispanic *cuecillos* (ceremonial graves). The top of the chapel spire of the Hacienda La Begoña can still be seen even at the reservoir's highest levels. During the dry season, in April or May, it has in some years been possible to walk or drive to the ruins of the old hacienda.

The Presa Ignacio Allende has a total capacity of 251 billion cubic meters, but for safety reasons the National Water Commission (CAN) permits a maximum volume of only 150 billion cubic meters. The dam has three floodgates; one is normally kept open for the irrigation of downstream farms, the other two gates can be opened if the Presa becomes too full. More than 20,000 acres of farmland are irrigated downstream. There is some boating activity, especially on weekends, with water-skiers and the occasional small sailboat, but the pollution of the reservoir makes swimming uninviting. A dozen fishermen make a part-time living fishing the Presa, catching carp and other whitefish from small homemade wooden skiffs. The government stocks the Presa with fish at regular intervals.

There are several other, much smaller presas around San Miguel. The first presa constructed in San Miguel, the "Presa del Obraje" is located below the Botanical Garden. First known as "Los Batanes," the dam was built in the early 17th century to allow watermills to function. The dam is located downstream from what was once a copious spring near the Landeta hacienda.

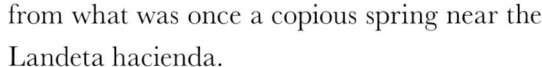

The higher dam, La Presa de las Colonias, is located near the entrance to the Botanical Garden. It was constructed in 1906. Rainwater, stored behind the dam, as well as water from the spring at Landeta was transported through a 3-foot diameter pipe to the Fábrica La Aurora textile mill where the water powered an electric generator.

A contract signed by the owner of the Landeta hacienda and the owners of the mill stipulated that "once the water has left the turbines at La Aurora, and entered the arroyo, the owners of La Aurora shall not be allowed to stop the flow of water to said arroyo by means of dams or any similar device, but will have to let it flow freely once it leaves the turbine." And so a San Miguel enterprise became an early pioneer in the use of hydro-electricity in Mexico.

Several communities in the municipio have small ponds that allow irrigation of crops but are naturally dependent on the seasonal rains. Because the water level of the aquifer has lowered steadily, most springs around San Miguel have dried up.

The Pyramid and Sanctuary at La Cañada de la Virgen

About 15 miles southwest of San Miguel, several miles off the road to Guanajuato, are an archeological site and a nature preserve, both called La Cañada de la Virgen (The Glen of the Virgin).

The 40-acre ceremonial center consists of several structures, including two pyramids, the highest of which is about 50 feet tall. Between 950—1150 A.D. the pre-Hispanic Toltecan society of what is now the municipio of San Miguel underwent a cultural development which reached extraordinary levels in the fields of architecture, stonemasonry, agriculture, ceramics, and commerce. This culture was linked to the great cities of Tula and Teotihuacan. Towards the year 1200 A.D. the area was abandoned, whether due to political power struggles or climatic change is unknown. Hunter-gatherer groups, generally referred to as Chichimecas, then roamed the area for more than 300 years until the arrival of the Spaniards.

The archeological restoration of the site, which had been looted repeatedly, began in 1995 under the direction of INAH, Mexico's National Institute of Anthropology and History. A small museum and visitor center is planned and public access is expected to be possible in the early decade of 2010.

An enormous privately owned Sanctuary surrounds the archeological site. A working horse-breeding and cattle ranch, it also offers educational facilities and ecological tourism. The incredibly diverse flora and fauna of the Preserve that still exists today range from the semi-arid to the sub-tropical.

The Sanctuary is open by appointment only to small groups. Hiking, horseback excursions, and ecological car tours are available. Picnics or ranch-style lunches can be provided. Visitors are expected to sign a "Wilderness Ethics Agreement" that establishes a two-way relationship between the visitor and nature.

The Sanctuary's website is www.canadadelavirgen.com.

The Big Tree at La Huerta

About eight miles south of San Miguel, along the banks of the Río Laja, is the village of *La Huerta* (The Orchard). It is reached via an abandoned railroad track and a quarter-mile long, 15-foot wide tunnel (dug in 1903) that begins near the Presa de Allende dam and follows the river for about four miles to a bridge across to the village, where many of the people earn their living making baskets from the reeds found along the river. La Huerta, however, is best known for having one of the biggest trees in Mexico, *taxodium mucronatum*, the Montezuma baldcypress, locally called *Sabino* or *ahuehuete* ("old man of the water" in Náhuatl). It is thought to be about 500 years old. Located near the middle of the village on top of a spring (which botanists credit for the huge size of the tree), it is easily reached via a narrow, marked path. The tree is about 70 feet high, the trunk 80 feet in circumference and about 25 feet in diameter. It is a cool, shady spot for a picnic. The Montezuma baldcypress is the national tree of Mexico.

A Few Hot Springs and a Cool Pool

Many hotels in San Miguel have pools and allow non-guests to swim, but there are a half dozen swimming pools and hot springs just a few miles from San Miguel on and off the highway to Dolores Hidalgo. All are within a few miles of each other and are open during daylight hours year-round. All sell snacks and soft drinks. The most popular balnearios are:

Taboada is about three miles north of town, then left for two miles on a cobblestone road has an Olympic-size pool and a water temperature of 111 degrees F.

Xoté, near Taboada, is mostly designed for children, with five small pools, water slides, and a playground.

La Gruta, is about 5 miles north of town, great for children, but not well-suited for exercise swimming. There are five small pools and a grotto at the end of a nearly 100-foot long tunnel. Water temperatures hover around 104 degrees F. There is a restaurant on the site.

Escondido Place, on the highway just before La Gruta, has nine pools of varying size and shape, with several connected grottos, and water temperatures around 104 degrees F.

Santa Verónica, on the road to Dolores about three miles north of town, is preferred by serious swimmers, has a large pool, with a cooler (86 degrees F.) water temperature.

Indian Chapels in the *Campo*

There are more than 300 churches and chapels within the municipio, the county, of San Miguel de Allende. About one-fourth are abandoned or completely in ruins. None are more than about ten miles from the Jardín. Most, of course, are found in or near the more than 500 communities surrounding the city, but dozens of abandoned chapels are located in difficult to reach locations.

The many primitive Indian chapels in the campo around San Miguel display curious representations of saints, crosses, and pagan symbols. The building of these chapels, known as the "*Calvarios de la Conquista*," was authorized by Royal Decree, requested by prominent Indian chieftains, Spanish conquerors, and missionaries. Spain was only too eager to accede to the pleas of the natives, realizing that it was to her own benefit. It was one way of obtaining the religious and political loyalty of the people. Here the Indian would be free from Spanish oppression and he could worship, in his own way, his sacred images, and revive his ancient rites. And although Catholic liturgy and ritual dazzled the Indians and filled a visual need, they managed to dilute, mix, fuse and disguise traces of their own rich religious heritage and graft them unto the new religion.

In front of each of these chapels one generally finds a small *calvario* (after Mt. Calvary), a doorless niche with a flat or vaulted ceiling. Within it stand crosses and floral offerings or candles. The "*calvario*" is a shrine dedicated to the souls of the departed spirits.

These vernacular structures show the same craftsmanship, creativity, the same devotion, discipline, and creativity as the better-known (and larger) churches in the town. The friars often permitted the Indians to add pre-Hispanic decorations and symbols to the façades. Sometimes these façades display a curious mixture of pagan and pre-Christian elements.

It is possible during a day-long excursion to visit dozens of these structures, but a knowledgeable guide and (during the rainy season) a four-wheel-drive vehicle are necessary.

The Sanctuary of Atotonilco

Eight miles northwest of San Miguel is the shrine of Atotonilco, a UNESCO World Heritage Site since 2008. Atotonilco in Náhuatl means "place of hot waters" and there are many thermal springs in its vicinity. Father Luis Felipe Neri Alfaro, a priest at the Oratorio had become concerned: "This spot has been a place of lawlessness and sensuality," he wrote. "Under the pretext of healthful bathing there have been contests, music, feasts, games, and other sins."

In 1740 construction was begun on the Santuario de Jesús el Nazareno de Atotonilco, a spiritual retreat where people could purge themselves of their sins. Construction was finished by 1748; several chapels were added in later years. The interior is covered with paintings of a multitude of divine and human personages, and inscriptions, poems and sonnets of a mystical nature, written by Alfaro. The simple, primitive, and naive paintings were made by Miguel Antonio Martínez de Pocasangre, about whom almost nothing is known. The paintings are murals, not frescos and the paint is tempera.

Behind the shrine is a large building, *La Casa de Ejercicios Espirituales* (The House of Spiritual Exercises), which is visited throughout the year by thousands of penitents for week-long retreats.

On the right side of the sanctuary in a glass case is an icon of Christ known as "*El Señor de la Columna.*" The statue, among the most venerated in Mexico, is carried during an all-night pilgrimage to the church of San Juan de Dios in San Miguel two weeks before Easter.

On September 16, 1810, Father Miguel Hidalgo and Ignacio Allende and their ragtag army stopped at Atotonilco and fetched a banner with the image of the Virgin of Guadalupe, which became the standard for the army of the Independence Movement.

Dolores Hidalgo, Cradle of Independence

Dolores Hidalgo, 25 miles northwest of San Miguel, with a population of about 60,000, is an important historic site since it was here that the War of Independence was begun on September 16, 1810. It is also one of the important ceramic centers of Mexico. It was an Otomí Indian settlement called Cocomacán until 1570, when the viceroy of New Spain officially declared the village the Congregación de Nuestra Señora de los Dolores, (Congregation of Our Lady of Sorrows). In 1826 the name was changed to Dolores Hidalgo, after Miguel Hidalgo y Costilla, the village priest and one of leaders of the War of Independence and is officially known as the "Cradle of Independence."

The shady Plaza Principal in the center of Dolores has a large statue of Hidalgo that dominates the square. The parish church that fronts the plaza, begun in 1712 but not finished till 1778, has a beautiful Churrigueresque façade. The steps in front of the church were the site of the Grito de Dolores (Shout or Cry of Dolores) that signalled the start of the rebellion. Also on the Plaza is La Casa de Visitas, a magnificent building dating from 1786. There are several other buildings and churches near the Plaza that are worth a visit. The Museo de la Independencia Nacional dates from the 18th century and was once the city's jail. The Museo Casa Hidalgo is located just a block from the Plaza. Father Hidalgo lived here from 1804-1810.

In an interesting change from the common method of naming streets in Mexico after saints or heroes, most of the streets in the center of Dolores are named after the 31 Mexican states.

A curious attraction in Dolores is the variety of ice creams sold on the main plaza, with flavors as exotic as alfalfa, beer, cheese, corn, honey, avocado, tequila, shrimp, mole, and yes, tuna (which is the flower of the *nopal* cactus).

The production of high quality ceramics is the largest industry, with several hundred workshops producing the famous Talavera ceramics. Many of the workshops allow visitors to watch the craftsmen at work.

The City of Santiago de Querétaro

Perhaps the most historic city in Mexico is Querétaro, an hour's drive from San Miguel. It was founded as Santiago de Querétaro on July 25, 1531, about ten years before San Miguel. The city has figured in important political dramas, from plotting Mexico's independence from Spain to signing the disastrous Treaty of Guadalupe Hidalgo, ending the Mexican-American War and ceding half of Mexico to the United States. Rich in history and culture, Querétaro is especially noted for its colonial architecture. Although there has been considerable development of industry around the city in recent years, the old town has preserved much of the more tranquil atmosphere of the past. Parts of the center of the city are closed to traffic, making walking through its streets and plazas a delightful experience.

A nearly mile-long aqueduct, still functioning, was built between 1726 and 1738 by the Marqués de la Villa del Villar del Águila. Its 74 towering arches, some as high as 75 feet, carries water from a spring to the city.

The city has a number of remarkable churches, monasteries, and mansions; one of the loveliest is the home of La Corregidora, Doña Josefa Ortiz de Domínguez. The wife of the mayor, it was she who in effect launched Mexico's War of Independence. The plotters of the independence movement met from time to time at her house under the guise of discussing literary matters. When the plot was discovered, she secretly notified the rebels and so became one of Mexico's heroines.

It was to Querétaro that ill-fated, Austrian-born Emperor Maximilian fled with the remnants of his government in 1867, hoping to maintain his empire, although Napoleon had withdrawn nearly all French troops from Mexico earlier that year. Maximilian surrendered to Benito Juárez, was court-martialed, and executed on June 9, 1867 on the Hill of the Bells, now a park not far from the city center.

In 1996 the historic center was named a UNESCO World Heritage Site.

The Abandoned Mining Town of Mineral de Pozos

Pozos (wells or mine shafts) is a nearly abandoned mining town less than an hour's drive from San Miguel. A hundred years ago, its miners and townsfolk numbered more than 40,000. Mining stopped when the 1910 Revolution began and has never resumed. Miners joined or were conscripted into the various fighting factions; foreign capital (many of the mines were operated by Europeans and Americans) dried up; without pumps, groundwater filled the mine shafts; spare parts for the mining machinery became unavailable; the silver market tanked (silver was one of many minerals that were mined). At one point in the late 1800s more than 300 mine sites were claimed.

The population now stands at fewer than 1,000. Its hundreds of ruins, both in the town and the mining areas flanking the ghost-town, are a favorite subject for painters and photographers. A number of motion pictures have used Mineral de Pozos as a location. In the last decade a dozen foreigners have settled in the town and remodeled old ruins while two bed and breakfast inns have opened. A few art galleries are open on weekends, and a small number of the inhabitants make a living fashioning reproductions of ancient pre-Hispanic musical instruments and ornaments.

In the mining area called Santa Brígida, two miles east of Pozos, three 50-feet high smelting ovens, built by Jesuits around 1597, are among the oldest structures in the State of Guanajuato. The mine area is open to the public as is the huge Cinco Señores mining concern a mile west of town.

For a short time (1896-1910) during the reign of the dictator Porfirio Díaz, the town was renamed Ciudad Porfirio Díaz.

Guanajuato, Hill of the Frogs

The city of Guanajuato, the capital of the state of Guanajuato, with a population of about 150,000, lies about 40 miles west of San Miguel de Allende. Founded in 1557, it is one of the most interesting and beautiful cities in Mexico. In the middle of the 16th century silver was discovered and the first silver mines opened, establishing the prosperity of the town. It is said that half of all the silver mined in the Americas came from Guanajuato. The town holds an important place in the history of Mexico, especially for the assault at the beginning of the War of Independence. It was for a short time also the capital of Mexico.

Guanajuato, whose name is derived from a Tarascan word meaning "Hill of Frogs," begins at the bottom of a gorge, sweeping up the surrounding hills in a tapestry of multicolored dwellings. More than five miles of tunnels under the city, excavated in the middle of the 20th century as a flood control measure, allows traffic to avoid the city's narrow streets.

In 1988 the city was designated a UNESCO World Heritage Site. Its rich cultural and intellectual life combines with the visual attractions of the cityscape to make Guanajuato one of the most popular tourist centers in Mexico. It is the site of the University of Guanajuato, which has an enrollment of more than 20,000 students.

Filled with small plazas, narrow alleys, including the famous *Callejón del Beso* (Alley of the Kiss) with only 27 inches (68 cm) between balconies, fascinating museums (among them the Diego Rivera Museum and the macabre Mummy Museum), and handsome churches, the city merits several days of sightseeing.

In October the city hosts the world-famous Cervantino Festival, which draws thousands from all over the world to its many cultural activities.

Visitors sometimes look around in awe at a city that seems to be built house-upon-house with such a variety of styles that it is difficult to accept its being called a "colonial" town. Regarding its unique physiognomy, local writer Jorge Ibargüengoitia once said: "The architecture of Guanajuato is easy to identify, but impossible to define."

A Calendar of Events

Cultural Events, Historic Festivities and Religious Celebrations

The Mexico Tourist Office mentions more than 5,000 celebrations. The Church insists there are more than 2,500 canonized saints. The Biblioteca Pública offers more than 1,500 lectures, films, plays, concerts and other events annually. No day seems to be without an event or celebration. In a country known for its fiestas, San Miguel de Allende has no equals.

The religious celebrations of *Semana Santa* (Holy Week), Corpus Christi (Body of Christ), and the Feasts of the Virgin of Loreto and San Miguel Arcángel, rank among the most impressive, while the Locos Parade in June draws the most (about 10,000) participants and spectators.

Special events occur often, and detailed information can be obtained from many sources, including *Atención San Miguel*, the weekly English language newspaper published on Fridays and by visiting the Tourist Office located on the Jardín. Bulletin boards in the churches display announcements of religious events, processions and pilgrimages.

Some religious events are subject to changes of date, often related to the timing of Easter. *Novenas*, for example, are devotions consisting of prayers or services on nine consecutive days preceding a saint's day. Therefore fireworks or other activities can take place many days before the actual celebration. Some happen the evening before the actual date. A particularly useful guide for these religious events is the annually published "Calendario del Más Antiguo Galván," an almanac with a remarkable amount of religious, astronomical, and other information, readily available in *librerías* (bookstores) in several of the churches.

January

January 1: *Año Nuevo* (New Year's Day). A legal holiday.

January 3: The birthday of two War of Independence heroes, both *sanmiguelenses*: Juan José de los Reyes Martínez Amaro, known as *Pípila*, and Juan Aldama, who was one of Allende's lieutenants. At 10 a.m. a civil ceremony is held on the atrium of the San Juan de Dios church.

January 6: *Día de los Santos Reyes* or *Día de los Tres Reyes Magos* (Three Kings Day) commemorates the Magi, the Three Wise Men, who followed the Star of Bethlehem to the manger and Jesus. A Bible story tells of Three Kings, Melchior, Gaspar, and Balthazar, who traveled for 12 days and nights and arrived in Bethlehem bearing gifts for the baby Jesus.

Twelve days after Christmas, Mexican children awake to find toys and gifts left for them by the Magi. Many children leave hay in their shoes for the camels, just as children north of the border might leave carrots for Santa's reindeer. The day is celebrated with a special treat —the *Rosca de Reyes* (Wreath of the Kings), a crown-shaped sweet cake decorated with candied cactus or fruit. A tiny plastic figure of a baby is hidden in the dough before baking, a representation of the hiding of the Christ Child from King Herod. Whoever gets the slice containing the little doll must host a party and provide the *tamales* and *atole* on Candelaria Day. (See February 2.) Candelaria marks the end of Mexico's Christmas season.

January 17: *Día de San Antonio Abad* (St. Anthony the Abbot Day). The blessing of the animals now seldom involves farm animals. These days it is more likely that cats, dogs, parrots, or goldfish and other pets are blessed. Blessings take place in the late afternoon, usually at the Oratorio or the Parroquia de San Antonio de Padua.

January 21: The official birthday of General José Ignacio María de Allende y Unzaga, who was born in 1769. (He was once thought to have been born on January 20 and a plaque on the front of his birthplace lists the date thus.) Floral wreaths are laid on the corner of the house he was born in, now the Museo Histórico de San Miguel de Allende, on the corner of Umarán and Cuna de Allende. At 9 a.m. a civic ceremony is held on the esplanade in front of the Parroquia. Military parades circle the downtown streets and speeches are made. Flags are flown at full-staff.

January 23: Pilgrims arrive in San Miguel from many directions to participate in the *perigrinación* to San Juan de los Lagos and are greeted by bells, dances, and fireworks.

January 24: After an early morning Mass at the Parroquia, thousands of pilgrims depart for the nine-day, 100-mile procession to San Juan de los Lagos in the state of Jalisco. There they worship at the shrine of the *Virgen de San Juan de los Lagos*, the second most venerated religious symbol (after the Virgin of Guadalupe) in Mexico. As many as three million people make the annual pilgrimage.

A Lent, Carnival, and Easter Schedule

Events related to Easter are movable and can take place over several months, beginning as early as February and ending as late as June.

It is impossible to attend all of San Miguel's Easter celebrations since many events overlap and occur at various locations. There is much duplication. Dates and times of the activities, processions, and Masses are listed on posters at the entrance to churches. Bear in mind that there are likely to be small changes of times and locations from year to year. Here follows a timeline:

Pascua (Easter) and the week preceding, *Semana Santa* (Holy Week) bring an astonishing array of activities and processions to San Miguel. In a city famed for the variety and number of fiestas and ceremonies, *Semana Santa* is second to none.

The dates for Easter (and thus Lent and other religious events) were arrived at through a complicated method which Church Fathers agreed on during the

First Council of Nicaea in 325 A.D. They decided that Easter Sunday should be celebrated on the Sunday after the first full moon on or after the Vernal Equinox. And so Easter cannot be earlier than March 22 or later than April 25, a span of 35 days.

Cuaresma (Lent) is the period of 40 days, from Ash Wednesday to Easter Sunday, that can begin as early as February 10 or as late as March 16. It is observed by the Roman Catholic Church (and some Protestant churches) as a time of penitence, reflection, and fasting. The period represents the time Christ spent in solitude in the wilderness. Lenten devotions are held in various churches, usually on Fridays. During Lent a choral Mass is celebrated every Friday morning at 9 a.m. in the Oratorio church. A boys' choir (with a few girls in attendance) performs the "Cantos de la Pasión," works of 19th century San Miguel composers.

Carnaval (Carnival) is a festival that marks the beginning of Lent, 49 days before Easter. Lent ends on Mardi Gras (lit. Fat Tuesday), the day before Ash  Wednesday. It may begin as early as February 3 or as late as March 9. Although several week-long colorful festivals take place in Mexico, principally in Mazatlán and Veracruz, Carnival is not celebrated in San Miguel except on the weekend and the Monday and Tuesday preceding Ash Wednesday. It is the custom for children to crack *cascarones* (eggshells filled with confetti) over the heads of people, friends and strangers alike, especially in the Jardín.

Miércoles de Ceniza (Ash Wednesday) marks the beginning of Lent. It is the day, 40 days before Easter (not counting Sundays), when ashes in the shape of a cross are applied to the foreheads of the faithful, signifying repentance. The ashes are from the burnt palm fronds used on Palm Sunday in the previous year.

Two weeks before Easter: At midnight of the Sunday two weeks before Easter, a highly venerated effigy, *Nuestro Señor de la Columna* (Our Lord of the Column), is carried in an impressive early morning procession from the Santuario de Atotonilco, eight miles from San Miguel, to the San Juan de Dios Church.

Thousands of pilgrims accompany the statue on its journey. The statue, portraying the flagellated Christ, is a life-size polychrome figure, made of wood and porcelain, of unknown origin and age (but most likely created in Mexico during the 18th century). The tradition dates back, it is believed, to 1812, when a plague threatened the population of San Miguel. In the hope that the statue would miraculously stop the plague, it was taken to the San Juan de Dios church, which adjoined the hospital.

The procession leaves Atotonilco at midnight. It is perhaps the most stirring procession of the year, a slow and solemn walk with frequent stops along the way. Images of St. John and the Virgin Mary accompany the bound figure of Christ. The figures are shrouded in hundreds of colored silk scarves and covered in a white manta to protect them en route. As it nears the town, stops are more frequent. Fragrant herbs—chamomile, fennel, rose petals and other flowers and oranges—are strewn on the road, while flower vases and arches line the route. The scarves are removed when the procession enters the Avenida Independencia to be greeted by the faithful with fireworks and balloons along the avenue and in the Plaza Garibaldi, whence it continues on Calle San Antonio Abad to the San Juan de Dios church, where a Mass is celebrated at 8 a.m.

Tuesday before Holy Week: *El Día del Divino Preso* (The Day of the Divine Prisoner) is the day when prisoners welcome family, enjoy a meal, and attend Mass at the state prison (*CERESO: Centro de Readaptación Social*) located on the outskirts of town.

Friday before Holy Week: The Friday nine days before Easter is called *Viernes de Dolores* (Friday of the Sorrows) and honors the mother of Christ. A special Mass is celebrated in the morning at the Oratorio. Images of the Holy Virgin are placed at the foot of the altar to be blessed, and then taken home to be displayed in a window or doorway with flowers and candles. These home-made altars are dedicated to the suffering of the Virgin Mary during Christ's Passion. A picture of the Virgin always occupies a central place. More of the faithful go to confession on this day than on any other, or so it is said. It is an old tradition, dating from the early 1700s, little observed in most of Mexico, but widely observed in the Bajío and much of the state of Guanajuato.

In early evening at the San Francisco church the rosary of the seven sorrows (*Corona Dolorosa*) of the Virgin is recited and figures of Christ, the Virgin Mary, and St. John are carried around the Stations of the Cross in the church, while a choir or the organ accompanies the procession. Gifts are offered by members of the Third Order of St. Francis and by other devout people.

At dusk candles are lit and visitors welcomed at many homes (and some commercial establishments) where elaborate altars are set up in windows, doorways, and patios. Traditionally, bitter oranges are used in the decoration, representing the tears of the Virgin. White flowers represent purity, purple flowers symbolize grief, and red flowers represent the blood shed by Jesus. Gold foil is used to represent the highest purity. Pots of sprouting wheat or fennel represent renewal and the resurrection of life. These tableaux are seen all over town but especially on Calles Correo, Sollano, Terraplén, Huertas, Barranca, and Chorro, and in the alleys leading from the Salida a Querétaro down the slope of the hill to Barranca and Chorro: Garita, Sierra, Montes de Oca, Piedras Chinas, and Garza. Some householders offer candy or cookies, others ices, popsicles or other snacks. Visits to these altars can go on till midnight.

In late afternoon many of the four dozen public fountains of the town are also lavishly decorated with fragrant herbs and flowers that symbolize different aspects of the sorrow of the Virgin, a custom begun when neighbors got together to clean and decorate the often-neglected fountains. By late evening or early morning many of the decorations are taken down to avoid theft or vandalism.

Sunday before Easter, Palm Sunday: *Domingo de Ramos* (Palm Sunday) brings several processions. At many churches, vendors show their elaborately woven palm

fronds, often decorated with flowers or bouquets of herbs. The custom refers to the strewing of palm leaves during the triumphant entry of Jesus into Jerusalem.

At midnight a Blessing of the Palms takes place on the Caracol (above Calle 5 de Mayo) and a few minutes after midnight a small procession begins and follows the Prolongación de Aldama, Cardo, and Callejón de San Antonio, ending at the Parroquia de San Antonio de Padua.

At 6:30 a.m. before the first Mass of the day, another Blessing of the Palms takes place in front of the Templo de la Salud church on the Plaza Cívica, after which a small procession goes on to the nearby Oratorio church. At 8 a.m. another Blessing of the Palms takes place at the Templo de la Salud.

At 10 a.m. after another Blessing at the Calvario chapel at the top of Calle San Francisco, a small procession—Christ on a burro, followed by the Twelve Apostles and other Biblical figures—moves toward the San Francisco church two blocks downhill where a Mass is celebrated shortly afterward.

At 10 a.m. a gathering also takes place in Parque Benito Juárez. A Blessing and a procession then follows at 10:30 a.m. and moves from the park along Calle Sollano to the Parroquia, where a Mass is celebrated.

Masses at the Oratorio and the Parroquia attract the biggest crowds. After Mass the priests bless the palms held aloft by the congregation. Before the 11 a.m. Mass at the Parroquia a small procession departs from Santa Escuela, the adjacent church, with a figure of Christ on a donkey, accompanied by several priests in red vestments. The procession moves up Calle Correo, thence Corregidora, to San Francisco, thence around the Jardín back to the church.

At the Parroquia de San Antonio de Padua two blocks southwest of the Instituto Allende, a Blessing of the Palms takes place at noon, after Mass. A small procession meanders around the streets of the barrio, ending at the church with another Mass.

At 5:30 p.m. the Blessing of the Palms (and a small procession) takes place at the San Juan de Dios church.

At 6:30 p.m. a small procession moves from the de la Salud church to the Oratorio.

At 7 p.m. an evening procession at the Oratorio features boys dressed as Apostles, singing songs of praise celebrating Christ's entrance into Jerusalem.

Holy Week: During Monday, Tuesday, and Wednesday of *Semana Santa*, considered the lesser days, dramatizations of the *Prendimiento*, the Arrest of Christ and the *Aposentillo* (Imprisonment) take place in various churches.

Monday before Easter: The Monday before Easter, *Lunes Santo*, the *Prendimiento*, the Arrest of Christ, and of the subsequent imprisonment, *Aposentillo*, is enacted in the morning at the Oratorio with Judas and Roman soldiers. A simulated jail is installed on the main altar.

Tuesday before Easter: During Tuesday of Holy Week, *Martes Santo*, a service is held in late afternoon at the Oratorio. The Arrest of Christ, the *Aposentillo*, is commemorated. About 30 boys and girls dressed in white and purple clothes offer incense and flowers.

Also in the late afternoon at 5 p.m. at the San Juan de Dios church, a procession carrying the image of *El Señor de la Columna* takes place. It follows this route: Calles San Rafael, San Antonio Abad, Indio Triste, San Pedro, Canal, Beneficencia, Pilancón, San Antonio Abad, and then back to the church.

In many churches the Washing of the Feet of the Apostles takes place in late afternoon or early evening.

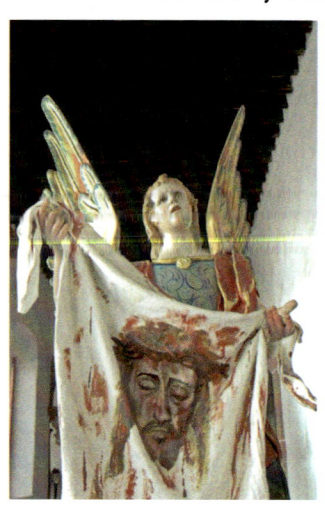

Wednesday before Easter: At 5 p.m. during Wednesday of Holy Week, *Miércoles Santo*, the Way of the Cross, *Via Crucis*, occurs at the Oratorio church. A dozen men carry an image of Jesus Christ, called *El Señor del Golpe*, on a platform decorated with flowers. The procession stops for short prayers at each of the 14 Stations of the Cross, stone niches set in the walls along the route. The procession makes a circular tour in the Centro, following Pepe Llanos, Mesones, Reloj, around the Plaza to Correo, Corregidora, San Francisco, Juárez, Mesones, to Núñez, to the Calvario chapel at the top of San Francisco, and then returns to the Oratorio. Most of the streets in Centro are closed to traffic.

At 5 p.m. the image of *El Señor de la Columna* is again carried around the San Juan de Dios neighborhood.

At 6 p.m. bread and wine are blessed in the San Francisco church

At 8 p.m. the Arrest of Christ (*Prendimiento*) is also reenacted at the San Rafael (Santa Escuela) church.

Thursday before Easter: *Jueves Santo*, called Maundy Thursday in English, is dedicated to giving to the poor.

A *Via Crucis* takes place in the San Antonio neighborhood, beginning at 10 a.m.

After 5 p.m. the town becomes eerily silent, as bells will not be rung until late Saturday evening.

At 5 p.m. a recreation of the Ceremony of the Washing of the Feet of the Disciples (*Lavatorio*) is featured at several churches, including the Oratorio, de la Salud, and the Parroquias of San Miguel Arcángel and San Antonio de Padua. The same ceremony takes place around 6 p.m. at the San Francisco church. During these ceremonies children represent the 12 disciples.

At 7:30 p.m. a reenactment of the *Prendimiento* takes place in the atrium of the Parroquia de San Antonio de Padua.

The Santa Ana church next to the Biblioteca Pública features a beautifully decorated altar and a life-size image of the crucified Christ lying at the base of the altar. The image is touched with reverence while the faithful file by. A Mass commemorating the Last Supper is celebrated in most churches. After 6 p.m. many of the faithful will visit seven churches, an Italian custom dating from the 16th century and easy to accomplish among the many churches and chapels in San Miguel.

Friday before Easter: Good Friday, *Viernes Santo*, the day when the death of Christ on the cross is commemorated, features several processions and tableaux. Except for the sound of the bells in the clock-tower, all remains quiet. Around 8 a.m. villagers from Atotonilco bring a huge wooden cross to the Parroquia. It

belonged to Father Luis Felipe Neri de Alfaro, the priest who built the Atotonilco Sanctuary and several of the religious buildings in San Miguel.

Also at 8 a.m. a small procession leaves the tiny chapel on Piedras Chinas called El Oratorio de Los Siete Dolores de la Purísima Virgen and meanders through nearby streets and alleys.

At 10 a.m. *El Señor de la Columna* is carried around from the San Juan de Dios church to the Parroquia, where it is displayed through Easter.

Also at 10 a.m. a lengthy *Via Crucis* procession takes place in the San Antonio neighborhood, beginning at its church, the Parroquia de San Antonio de Padua. The route follows Calle Héroes, 20 de Enero Norte, Orizaba, Refugio Norte, San Jorge, San Elias, San Rafael, San Martín, 28 de Abril Sur, La Luz, 20 de Enero Sur, Tinajitas, and ends at the Plaza San Antonio.

At 11 a.m. a moot court is set up on the steps of Santa Escuela (the church next to the Parroquia) and the trial of Jesus, with Pontius Pilate presiding, is recreated. Pontius Pilate washes his hands; Roman soldiers stand guard on the roof of the church; Christ is led away. At 11:30 there follows the *Santo Encuentro y Paso del Sacerdote* (the Sacred Encounter and the Passing of the Priest), a procession begun in 1756 by Father Alfaro, the founder of the Atotonilco Sanctuary.

The procession begins at the Parroquia, guided by Father Alfaro's original banner and an 18th century statue of San Roque. Hundreds of parishioners including children dressed as angels take part. Barefoot penitents wearing crowns of thorns and tunics of rough cloth and bearing skulls or crosses are followed by Roman soldiers and four men carrying a statue of the Lord of Ecce Homo. The priest of the Parroquia follows, carrying a cross. The two thieves crucified alongside Christ flank the priest. There follows a statue of Jesus the Nazarene (kept on the main altar of Santa Escuela) that is carried on a bier by 22 men. Other statues on flower-laden litters follow: St. John, Mary Magdalene, Mary Cleofas (probably Mary's sister-in-law), Mary, the mother of Jesus, and Verónica, bearing the Holy Shroud with which she is believed to have cleansed the sweat and blood from Christ's face.

The route of the procession is short; the pace slow; its duration long. The procession leaves the Parroquia, then moves along the first block of Correo, turns on

Corregidora, then turns on San Francisco and ends back at the Parroquia after circling the Jardín.

When the procession returns to the Parroquia, the Sacred Encounter takes place between Jesus and his mother, whose statue is normally kept at the main altar of the Parroquia. Spectators are astonished when Jesus raises his head and looks at his mother. (A special mechanism, activated by a hidden rope, allows Christ's head to move.)

From noon until 3 p.m. priests in many churches, taking turns, deliver a sermon on the *Siete Palabras*, the Seven Last Words spoken by Christ on the cross. After the sermon, a procession circles the streets of the Centro.

At 5 p.m. the *Santo Entierro*, the Holy Burial, the longest and most solemn procession departs from the Oratorio. This procession has been repeated in San Miguel for almost 300 years. More than 1,000 parishioners participate.

A crucifix called the Lord of Inspiration leads the procession. It is carried by six men, and a group of 24 athletic men dressed as Roman soldiers march behind. They are followed by young girls, dressed in white with purple ribbons, who carry figures of small angels. Six groups of six women each—dressed in black, heads covered with black lace mantillas and an ornamental comb— carry the figures of the six archangels; more women dressed in black and carrying lanterns surround them. Next a glass catafalque containing a statue of the body of Jesus is borne by 36 men in black suits, accompanied by lantern bearers. The casket is followed by three priests, who walk under a gold and purple canopy. More women bearing the figure of the *Virgen de la Soledad* follow. Finally, the figures of the apostle John, Mary Magdalene, Nicodemus, and Joseph of Arimathea mark the closure of the procession.

The procession makes a clock-wise circle through the streets of Pepe Llanos, Juárez, San Francisco, Jardín, Hidalgo, and Mesones, and back to the Oratorio.

Saturday before Easter: On the Saturday before Easter, known as *Sábado Santo y de Gloria*, no Mass or Communion is celebrated before evening. At 3 p.m. many of the bells in town are rung to announce the death of Jesus.

A procession emerges around 9 p.m. from the Oratorio and follows Insurgentes, Reloj, Mesones, and Pepe Llanos. Women dressed in black, wearing white

gloves, participate in the procession, carrying the Virgin's black velvet train in total silence. The mourners give their condolences (*pésames*) to the Virgin Mary. Married women carry the statue on a bier while single women hold the Virgin's mantle.

Around 10 p.m. a vigil is enacted at the Oratorio, San Francisco, and other churches. Parishioners are asked to bring candles. At 10 p.m. the *Fuego Nuevo*, the New Fire, is enacted at the Oratorio and a candlelight vigil ceremony takes place at the San Antonio church. A Mass called the *Misa de Gloria* is celebrated at the Parroquia at 10 p.m.

Fireworks and bell ringing are supposed to begin at midnight, but since this is Mexico often start earlier.

Easter Sunday: *Domingo de Pascua* or *Domingo de Resurreción* ends Holy Week. There are early Masses in every church, seven in the Parroquia alone. At noon,  in front of the *Ex-Presidencia*, the former City Hall, the Burning of the Judases begins. Various organizations and businesses donate life-size effigies made of *papier mâché* which are strung from wires between the old city hall and the Jardín. Small rockets are attached to the figures, which may represent public figures and popular cartoon characters. Dozens of effigies are exploded with loud noises and smoke amid great excitement. Boys scramble to obtain body parts as trophies.

At first, the burning of effigies, which in a different form had originated in Spain during the occupation by the Moors, helped missionaries teach the Gospel to the Indians, specifically the Apostle Judas's betrayal. As the meaning of the event changed to reflect more political references, the government tried, without success, to ban the proceedings. The event is over in an hour.

First Wednesday after Easter: Although Holy Week is over, a related event follows: In late evening on Wednesday after Easter, the statue of *El Señor de la Columna* is shrouded again and taken at midnight from its temporary location at the San Juan de Dios church and returned to the *Santuario de Atotonilco* on the shoulders of the men who brought it to San Miguel two weeks before Easter. Fireworks are exploded along the route and at 3 a.m. at the chapel of *La Cruz del Perdón* on the road to Dolores, halfway to Atotonilco, a Mass is celebrated.

Thursday after Trinity Sunday: The day of the Feast of *Corpus Christi* (Latin, "body of Christ") is one of the most important religious celebrations in San Miguel and marks the end of Easter. (Trinity Sunday occurs eight weeks after Easter Sunday.) Thus Corpus Christi can take place as early as 21 May or as late as 24 June.

After a 6 p.m. Mass at the Parroquia, a procession with children dressed in white, accompanied by music, flowers, and sometimes fireworks, leaves the Parroquia around 7 p.m. and follows Calles Correo, Corregidora, San Francisco, Reloj, Mesones, and Hidalgo and returns to the parish church, visiting altars along the way set up in several San Miguel homes. The Holy Host, adorned with flowers, is carried behind the children by 20 men. More than four dozen men and women carrying lamps follow the procession. About 20 altars are visited at the homes of some of the oldest families in San Miguel.

February
Movable Events:
First Monday: *Día de la Constitución* (Constitution Day), nominally held on February 5, is a legal holiday to celebrate the promulgation of the Constitutions of 1857 and 1917. The holiday is now celebrated on the first Monday of February, in order to provide a long weekend. Banks, government offices and many businesses are closed. Flags are flown at full-staff.

February 2: *Día de la Candelaria* (Candlemas Day) celebrates the purification of the Virgin Mary after giving birth to Jesus and the presentation of Jesus in the temple, 40 days after his birth. *Candelaria* is also linked to a pre-Hispanic tradition, the Blessing of the Seeds. *Campesinos* from some rural farming communities bring seeds for the next season's crop to be blessed at a morning Mass at the Oratorio church. It is the first day of a huge plant and flower fair simply called *"Candelaria,"* celebrated in San Miguel for a week or so in Parque Benito Juárez.

It is also, coincidentally, New Year's Day on the Aztec calendar. Nearly a hundred nursery vendors from many parts of Mexico participate. The event signals the unofficial start of spring. The fair, first held in the Jardín but moved to the park in 1990, is a blend of religious and community celebrations. In recent years the fair has included many cultural events with music, dance performances, and (after dark) movies.

February 5: Actual anniversary of the promulgation of the Constitutions of 1857 and 1917. (See First Monday, above.) At 10 a.m. a civic ceremony takes place in the Jardín.

February 14: Anniversary of the death of Vicente Guerrero, a hero of the independence movement, in 1831. Flags are flown at half-staff.

February 14: *Día de San Valentín* (Valentine's Day), sometimes called Friendship Day (*Día de la Amistad*).

February 19: *Día del Ejército Mexicano* (Mexican Army Day). Flags are flown full-staff and military parades are staged.

February 22: Anniversary of the deaths of President Francisco I. Madero and Vice President José María Pino Suárez, who were murdered in 1913. Flags are flown at half staff.

February 24: *Día de la Bandera* (Flag Day). At 10 a.m. civil ceremonies take place at the Plaza de los Héroes (the Mirador on the Salida a Querétaro), and flags, of course, are flown at full-staff.

February 28: Anniversary of the death of the Aztec Emperor Cuauhtémoc in 1525. Flags are flown at half-staff.

March
Movable Events:

First Friday: *Festividad del Señor de la Conquista* (Feast of the Lord of the Conquest). The first Friday in March is set aside in San Miguel for the veneration of a statue of the crucified Christ that is kept in a niche in the Parroquia, but is moved on this day to the high altar in the church. An early Mass is celebrated in the Parroquia and afterward hundreds of Indian *conchero* dancers in extravagant feathered costumes perform their rituals and dances on the esplanade in front of the church and around the Jardín.

Religious celebrations and fireworks actually begin the night before. During the celebration the faithful recite 33 prayers—one for each year of the life of Jesus.

It is thought that the statue, known as *Nuestro Señor de la Conquista* (Our Lord of the Conquest) was brought to San Miguel a few years after its founding. The statue, made of cornstalks, rope, orchid paste, and a glue made from orchid bulbs and sugar cane pulp, much like papier mâché and thus very light, was made in Pátzcuaro and brought to San Miguel in the late 16th century. Indigenous dancers, called *Danzantes Concheros Chichimecas*, who represent some of the original tribes who dominated this area 500 years ago, along with hundreds of the faithful from nearby communities, come to honor the figure that represents the Catholic roots of the rural com-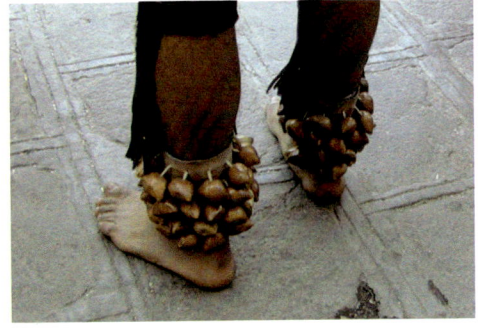munities. The *conchero* dancers (named after the *concha*, or shell of the armadillo, and resembling a mandolin) wear costumes of brightly colored and decorated animal skin or cloth, with seed-pod rattles on their ankles and wrists, as well as elaborate headdresses made of peacock, turkey, rooster, or pheasant feathers.

"*Conquista*" does not denote "conquest" or "subjection," but the triumph of conversion to Christianity. The dancers are worshippers, not performers.

Sunday after the First Friday: Celebrations for *El Señor de la Conquista* in the village of San Miguel Viejo, the site of the first settlement of San Miguel de los Chichimecas, a few miles west of town.

Third Monday: Commemoration of the birthday of Benito Juárez, Mexico's beloved president, who was born on March 21 in 1806. In order to give citizens a long weekend, it is celebrated on the third Monday of March. Flags are flown at full-staff. It is a national holiday. Parades are held around the Jardín and fireworks are launched after dark.

Friday nearest the Spring Equinox: Children's Spring Parade. Thousands of kindergarten students parade at mid-morning from El Portón, the intersection of Calzada de la Luz and Calle Hidalgo, through the streets in Centro, to end up at the Jardín. The colorful celebration of spring, *primavera*, features small children dressed up as flowers, butterflies, birds, and cartoon or fairytale characters. In a town known for its parades and processions, this is perhaps the most charming.

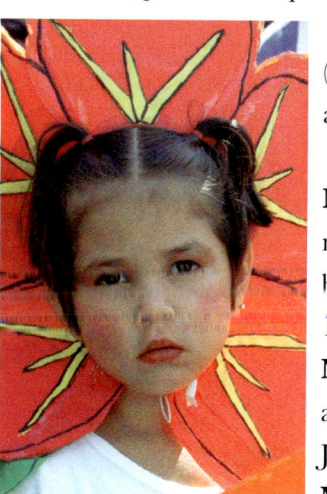

Last week in March: The *Festival de Música Barroca* (Baroque Music Festival) features concerts, master classes, and lectures.

March 1: *Aniversario de la Proclamación del Plan de Ayutla* (Anniversary of the Proclamation of the Plan of Ayutla), the beginning of the liberal rebellion against Santa Anna, in 1854. Flags are flown at full-staff.

March 8: *Día de San Juan de Dios*, patron saint of the sick and of hospitals. St. John's Day is celebrated at the San Juan de Dios church with a Mass and fireworks.

March 17: St. Patrick's Day. A number of people in the expatriate community celebrate loudly, while others only wear green items of clothing. A small statue of St. Patrick can be found in the Parroquia.

The Great Irish Famine in the 19th century claimed a million lives and forced two million hungry Irish immigrants to flee to America. Many joined the U.S. Army. One-fourth of all enlisted men in the U.S. Army were born in Ireland. During the Mexican-American War of 1846-1848 a small contingent of Irish soldiers deserted and joined the Mexican side, repulsed by the idea of fighting in a Catholic country. The battalion became known as "San Patricios." They carried a green (what else!) banner adorned with a harp, with the motto Erin Go Bragh (Ireland Forever) and the image of St. Patrick, the patron saint of Ireland. Most of the battalion of nearly 800 soldiers were killed, wounded, or taken prisoner in various battles in northern Mexico. In 1847, at the Battle of Churubusco, the battalion suffered heavy losses. More than 80 were captured, 72 court-martialed, and 50 executed.

The San Patricios are revered by Mexicans who believe that the Irish defected solely on the issue of religion. American history contends that the religious bond was not the main reason for the defections from the U.S. Army. It cites other reasons, among them religious prejudice against Catholics, lack of promotion for foreign-born soldiers, cruel punishments for even the slightest infractions, and, above all, enticements offered by the Mexican government of higher pay, land grants, and higher rank. The Patricios are commemorated each year on September 12.

March 18: *Aniversario de la Expropiación Petrolera* (Anniversary of the Nationalization of the Petroleum Industry) in 1938. Flags are flown at full-staff.

March 19: *Festividad de San José* (St. Joseph's Day). On the night before the saint's day a procession leaves from the Capilla de San José (on the top of the Cuesta de San José) and makes its way to the Oratorio, where a special Mass is celebrated and the many San José figures carried in the procession are blessed. There are also dances at the Obraje chapel. San José is the husband of the Virgin Mary.

March 21: It is the actual anniversary of the birth of Benito Juárez, Mexico's beloved president. It is now celebrated on the third Monday of the month. Some still celebrate it on this day. At 10 a.m. a civil ceremony takes place at Parque Benito Juárez. Flags are flown at full-staff.

March 26: *Promulgación del Plan de Guadalupe* (Promulgation of the Guadalupe Plan), a political document, during the Revolution. Flags are flown at full-staff.

April
Movable Events:
First Sunday in April: In Mexico Daylight Savings Time (*Horario de Verano*) begins at 2 a.m. Clocks are set ahead one hour.
After Easter, usually in April: The week-long *Festival Internacional de Títeres*, the International Puppet Festival. (www.festivaldetiteres.com)

April 2: Anniversary of the Fall of Puebla in 1867. Flags are flown at full-staff.
April 10: Anniversary of the death of Emiliano Zapata in 1919. Flags are flown at half-staff.
April 21: Anniversary of the heroic defense of the port of Veracruz in 1914. Flags are flown at half-staff.
April 30: *Día del Niño* (Day of the Child). Children are honored with gifts and parties.

May
Movable Events:
First Sunday: *Fiesta de la Santa Cruz* in the Guadiana neighborhood.
Second Sunday: *Fiesta de la Santa Cruz* in the Ojo de Agua neighborhood.
Third Sunday: *Fiesta de la Santa Cruz* in the Palmita neighborhood.
Last week and last weekend: Weeklong *Santa Cruz* celebrations begin in Valle del Maíz with parades, dances, musical performances, mock battles, and an abundance of fireworks.

May 1: *Día Internacional del Trabajo* (International Labor Day). It is a legal holiday in Mexico with a parade of workers and school children. Flags are flown at full-staff.

May 2: Commemoration of the deaths of the pilots of the Mexican Expeditionary Air Force, *Escuadrón 201*, in the Philippines in 1945. Flags are flown at half-staff.

May 3: *Día de la Santa Cruz* (Holy Cross Day) commemorates the finding of the

Cross by St. Helen, the mother of the Emperor Constantine the Great. It is a day devoted to builders and masons. Altars or crosses that are blessed during an early morning Mass are erected on most construction sites. Employers are expected to provide food, and, especially, drink for the workers. No work gets done...

May 5: *Cinco de Mayo* celebrations commemorate the major but temporary defeat of the French invading forces at the Battle of Puebla in 1862, when a small band of Mexican soldiers routed a French battalion twice its size. This holiday is celebrated more in the U.S. than in Mexico. In Mexico it is an official holiday only for federal government employees and citizens of the city of Puebla. At 10 a.m. a civil ceremony is enacted in the Jardín. Flags are flown at full-staff.

May 8: The birthday, in 1753, of Father Miguel Hidalgo y Costilla. Flags are flown at full-staff.

May 10: *Día de la Madre* (Mother's Day), a fixed date in Mexico and a sort of unofficial holiday. Special Masses are held in honor of mothers who are often lavishly entertained at midday comidas.

May 15: *Día de San Isidro* (St. Isadore's Day). San Isidro is the patron saint of both rain and livestock. Cattle are often decorated and blessed by priests in some of the rural communities near San Miguel.

May 15: *Día del Maestro* (Teacher's Day). Teachers are honored in the schools with gifts, cards, and parties. A ceremony is held in the Jardín during which the teachers are thanked for their services.

May 15: Celebration of the taking of Querétaro by the Republican forces in 1867. Flags are flown at full-staff.

May 17: The feast day of San Pascual Bailón, a saint concerned with gardening, agriculture, and cooking. Celebrations are held in front of the San Antonio and Oratorio churches, with dances, music, and fireworks.

May 21: Anniversary of the death of Venustiano Carranza in 1920. Carranza was briefly the president of Mexico in 1914 and again from 1915-1920. Flags are flown at half-staff.

May 26: Fiesta of San Felipe Neri (1515-1595), founder of the Oratorio church in Rome and the patron saint of educators and humorists. The *oratorianos* lived in a community of spiritual instruction and entertainment for children and young people. In San Miguel it is celebrated early in the morning with fireworks in front of the Oratorio church and with music and dancing during the day. Many small *puestos* (stands) in front of the church sell (mostly) wooden toys for children.

June
Movable Events:
June 13, if a Sunday; if not, the following Sunday: The Locos Parade honors the feast day of San Antonio de Padua. The parade is a mixture of Christian and pagan traditions, a dancing and candy-throwing procession with extravagant costumes, many of which satirize past and present public figures. The traditions date back to the 18th century. It was originally a feast for San Pascual Bailón, the patron saint of field-and kitchen-workers. By dancing, the *hortelanos*, the orchard workers, gave thanks to their patron saint for the year's harvest. They wore scarecrow costumes and danced in circles. In deference to the saint, the laborers, usually men, decorated themselves with tools and other symbols of their trade, and the women adorned their clothing with kitchen utensils. The festivities were organized by various *cuadros* that consisted of extended family groups.

To keep participants and observers apart, specially designated participants were dressed as scarecrows. They wore grotesque costumes and masks, and often carried the desiccated remains of small animals. Their odd movements and appearances so startled observers that they earned the nickname *"locos"* (crazies). At some point in history, other roles appeared including that of clowns wearing paper or wooden masks, along with men dressed as women, called *"marotas"* (Amazons). Men often dressed as women, and women as men. (In 1731 the vice-

roy, Juan de Acuña, issued an edict forbidding the wearing of masks. The offense was punishable by 200 lashes and a fine of 200 pesos for Spaniards, and 200 lashes plus 2-3 months in jail for Indians.) But by the 19th century the *hortelanos* no longer dressed as scarecrows. Instead they began to wear imaginative costumes, clown masks, and harlequins with bright and flashy colors. Eventually the clowns and Amazons took the place of the field workers and kitchen workers, although the music of the *chirimía* (pipe), and the goatskin drum and the dance movements stayed the same. Brass bands soon appeared, playing popular music, including the cha-cha-cha and the danzón.

These days, the music is recorded and blares forth from speakers on the motorized floats. The parade is choreographed by four *cuadros* that organize the floats and the elaborately costumed participants. Each *cuadro* is subdivided into smaller groups, called *cuadrillas*, and each performs its own dance. More than 50 floats lead the parade, while as many as 10,000 people, onlookers and participants alike, revel in the sights and the sounds.

Today, candy has taken the place of the fruit, and the children shout *"Dulce! Dulce!"* ("Candy! Candy!") A dizzying variety of costumes is featured. Many of the costumes represent historical figures, politicians, and cartoon characters. There is still an interesting proclivity for men to dress up as women. Traditionalists remind us, though, that the "Locos Parade" is not a carnival, but a sacred fiesta in honor of San Pascual Bailón and San Antonio de Padua.

The hours-long parade starts at noon at Calle Cardo and eventually winds its way to the Jardín via the Ancha de San Antonio, Zacateros, Canal, Hernández Macías, Insurgentes, Pepe Llanos, Mesones, Núñez, and San Francisco. Many of the celebrations continue into the evening hours on the Plaza San Antonio with music, dancing, and fireworks.

If June 13 does not fall on a Sunday, San Antonio de Padua is nevertheless celebrated before sunrise with a lengthy and loud barrage of fireworks and rockets.

Third Sunday: *Día del Padre* (Father's Day).

June 1: *Día de la Marina Nacional* (National Navy Day). Flags are flown at full-staff.

June 21: Anniversary of the victory of the Nationalist forces over the Empire in 1867. Flags are flown at full-staff.

June 22: Birthday of Ignacio Ramírez, "El Nigromante," a writer, editor, and jurist who was born in San Miguel. A civil ceremony takes place in the Jardín and wreaths are placed in front of his house at Umarán 38.

June 24: *Natividad de San Juan Bautista* (Birthday of St. John the Baptist). A vigil for this saint begins the night before at the Oratorio church. He was once one of the town's six patron saints.

June 26: Anniversary of the death of Ignacio Allende. Flags are flown at half-staff and at 10 a.m. civic ceremonies are held in the Plaza Cívica.

July
Movable Events:
Last ten days: *Expresión en Corto*, an international short-film festival. The festival is a state-sponsored, nonprofit, cultural event that offers a variety of screenings, workshops, conferences, tributes, and activities at no cost to the visiting public. More than a thousand films from among nearly a hundred countries are received and hundreds shown at 20 different locations in San Miguel and Guanajuato (www.expresionencorto.com).

Third weekend: Fiesta at the Atotonilco Sanctuary. (See page xx.) The fiesta, honoring Jesús Nazareno, the patron of the Santuario, draws enormous crowds. There is music, fireworks, parades, and processions.

July 16: *Festividad de la Virgen del Carmen* (Feast of the Virgin of Carmen) launches a series of celebrations that will continue until the end of the month.

July 17: A *novena* (nine days of prayer) for Santa Ana begins with fireworks and ends on the saint's day, July 26.

July 17: Anniversary of the death of General Alvaro Obregón in 1928. Flags are flown at half-staff.

July 18: Anniversary of the death of Benito Juárez in 1872. Flags are flown at half-staff.

July 26: *Día de Santa Ana* (Feast of St. Anne). St. Anne, the grandmother of Jesus Christ, is honored at the Santa Ana church on Calle Insurgentes. A *novena* (nine days of prayer) began on July 17.

July 30: Anniversary of the death of Father Miguel Hidalgo y Costilla, who was executed in Coahuila in 1811. Flags are flown at half-staff.

August
Movable Events:

First two weeks: For more than 30 years the *Festival de Música de Cámara de San Miguel de Allende* (Chamber Music Festival) has been featuring performers from Mexico and around the world at the Ángela Peralta Theater (www.festivalsanmiguel.com).

August 8: *Festividad de Santo Domingo* (Feast of St. Dominic). St. Dominic Guzmán was the founder of the Dominican Order. The feast is celebrated with a Mass and a procession at the Santo Domingo church on the corner of Correo and the Salida a Querétaro.

August 9: The anniversary of the death in 1770 of Sor María Josefa Lina de la Canal y Hervás, who sponsored the building of the church and convent of La Concepción (Las Monjas).

August 15: *Festividad de Nuestra Señora de la Asunción* (Feast of the Assumption of the Blessed Virgin). It is celebrated at the church and convent of La Concepción (Las Monjas).

August 18: *Festividad de Santa Beatriz Meneses de Silva* (Feast of St. Beatrice). St. Beatrice founded the Congregation of the Immaculate Conception. The celebrations take place at the church and convent of La Concepción (Las Monjas).

August 22: *Día del Bombero* (Fireman's Day). A small parade featuring fire trucks and ambulances, all blaring their sirens, is held in early evening, followed by a Mass at the *Iglesia y Convento de la Concepción* (Las Monjas).

August 25: *Día de San Luis Rey* (Day of King St. Louis) is celebrated with great fanfare in the neighborhood of the same name a mile or so north of San Miguel.

August 28: María Santísima de la Salud is celebrated at the Templo de la Salud on the Plaza Cívica.

The *Fiestas Patrias* in September/October
Movable events:

Much of September and/or early October is devoted to the *Fiestas Patrias y Regionales*. Almost every day during these fiestas some activity or celebration takes place. There may be parades, processions, fireworks, concerts, or sporting events. The festivities include The Feast of the Virgin of Loreto, The Child Heroes Commemoration, the Independence Day celebrations, St. Michael's Day, the San Miguel Fair, and several others.

Early in September the schedule of events during the *Fiestas Patrias* is made available in the Tourist Office and posted on several billboards, while the religious events surrounding St. Michael's Day are posted in all of the churches. The newspapers, of course, also carry the information.

El Día de San Miguel is celebrated on September 29 if a Saturday, the following weekend if not. St. Michael is one of the three archangels mentioned by name in the Bible. The other two are St. Raphael and St. Gabriel (whose feast days are also September 29). St. Michael is mentioned twice in the Old Testament, appearing to Moses and Abraham. In paintings and sculptures he is usually shown with a scale (representing the weighing of souls) in one hand, a sword in the other,

slaying a dragon or the Devil. St. Michael is not only the patron saint of San Miguel de Allende, but also the patron saint of battle, the dead, grocers, mariners, police officers, paratroopers, and radiologists (!).

The *concheros* begin dancing at 10 a.m. in front of the Parroquia where at noon a Mass is celebrated. Dancing continues into the afternoon.

Thursday and Friday before the weekend, *conchero* dancers perform in the atrium of the Parroquia, usually in late morning or early afternoon. On the Friday evening before the feast day, fireworks are launched around 9 o'clock.

On Friday before the weekend celebrations a small procession, called the *Reseña de San Miguel* (Brief Account or Review), is held in late afternoon when several indigenous groups leave from the Calzada de la Aurora and the Puente de Guanajuato to meet at the corner of Calles Canal and Hidalgo, then proceed to the esplanade in front of the Parroquia.

Around 11:30 p.m., just before midnight, a parade with musical bands is marched through the main streets and the marchers prepare themselves to pick up the gunpowder that is to be used for the fireworks battle later in the night.

Saturday: At 1 a.m. on Saturday morning a group leaves the Jardín for Valle del Maíz to get the gunpowder.

At 3 a.m. on Saturday morning a barrage of rockets announces the arrival in the Jardín of the *mojigangas*, giant papier mâché figures. (The word *mojiganga* is variously translated as "farce," "burlesque," or "masquerade.")

At 4 a.m. the *Quema de Pólvora*, (the Burning of the Gunpowder) begins. It is the *Alborada*. Alborada can mean "Song of Dawn" or "Battle of Dawn." It is also sometimes translated as "reveille." It really doesn't matter, though. Thousands of rockets and fireworks are set off during a one-hour period. The battle between the archangel and the devil is on. St. Michael, of course, wins. After the fireworks, "*Las Mañanitas*," the Happy Birthday Song is sung to St. Michael.

The *Alborada* ceremony is not all that old. The tradition was started in 1924 by a group of textile workers from the Fábrica La Aurora. The festivities then, as now, involved music, fireworks, processions, and mojigangas, the giant *papier-mâché* puppets. That first celebration was such a success that the town fathers and the local clergy decided to incorporate the festivities into the celebrations of San Miguel's patron saint, and so the following year, on September 29, 1925, the first *Alborada* to San Miguel was held. This explains the involvement of the

people of Colonia Aurora in the festivities, especially the late afternoon procession, when a young boy dressed as San Miguel, rides on a float decorated with flowers, accompanied by children dressed as little angels.

At 6 a.m. "*Las Mañanitas,*" is sung again in front of the Parroquia.

At 9 a.m. Indian conchero dancers begin.

At 11:30 a.m. a Mass is celebrated to honor the saint at the Parroquia.

At noon a cavalcade of more than a hundred horsemen arrive for an outdoor Mass in front of the Parroquia.

Around 1 p.m. the *Quema de los Monitos* (Burning of the Figurines— *papier mâché* figures) takes place on the esplanade in front of the Parroquia.

After the Burning of the Figurines the *Voladores de Papantla*, the fliers from Veracruz, perform their sensational ceremony. A solemn homage to the Four Winds is performed on a tiny platform at the top of a 70-foot pole with chanting and flute music. The ropes are loosened and the fliers take off head-first on their downward flight. They usually give four performances throughout the afternoon and evening.

At 4 p.m. the *Encuentro de Ánimas* takes place at the Plaza de la Estación, and moves to the Puente de Guanajuato bridge at the end of Calle Canal. Then the dancers with their *xúchiles* parade through the streets to the Jardín. Over forty contingents of dancers, both local troupes and indigenous dance groups from all parts of Mexico take part.

At 5 p.m. the procession, having proceeded up Calle Canal, arrives in the Plaza. The Fiesta Queen leads the procession, followed by more mojigangas and dancers.

At 6 p.m. the *xúchiles* are delivered to the Parroquia. The *xúchiles* (from *xóchitl*, the Náhuatl word for "flower") are made in several colonias and rural communities, among them Valle del Maíz, Las Cuevitas, San Miguel Viejo, Alonso Yáñez, and Cruz del Palmar. Some of these constructions, 20 feet high and weighing as much as 1,200 pounds, are carried by a dozen men. The *xúchiles* are made of *cucharilla*, spoon-shaped plant material from the base of a cactus, a bamboo-like reed called *carrizo* and decorated with marigolds. The *concheros* continue dancing until well into the evening.

At 8 p.m. another Mass is celebrated in the Parroquia, usually by a bishop.

At 9 p.m. more fireworks and rockets are launched.

Sunday: Early Sunday morning (around 7 a.m.) the Indian dancers start up again.

At 11 a.m. a parade, with decorated trucks, music bands, and regional dancers, starts from the Ancha de San Antonio and heads for the Parroquia.

At 1 p.m. homage is paid to the founder of the city, Fray Juan de San Miguel at his monument, with a parade of mojigangas and conchero dancers.

After 1 p.m. there is music in the Jardín and the *Voladores de Papantla* perform several more times in the afternoon.

At 4 p.m. a bullfight takes place in the *Plaza de Toros Oriente* on Calle Recreo.

At 7 p.m. the Voladores perform their ceremony again.

At 9 p.m. fireworks take place in the Jardín.

The Sunday following the Feast Day of San Miguel marks the beginning of the *Octavas*, eight days of processions during which the statue of San Miguel is moved from the Parroquia to a number of other churches, first going to La Concepción (Las Monjas), then to the Oratorio and finally to the San Francisco church. The processions are accompanied by musicians and dancers.

September 8: *Festividad de la Virgen de Loreto* (Feast of the Virgin of Loreto). This is one of the most important religious celebrations in San Miguel. The festivities begin at the Oratorio before dawn with a singing of "*Las Mañanitas.*" The Virgin of Loreto is one of the incarnations of the Virgin Mary, the mother of Christ. She was once also one of the town's patron saints. The chapel, *La Santa Casa de Loreto*, a replica of the famous Holy House in Loreto, Italy, was built by Manuel Tomás de la Canal and is in the left transept of the Oratorio church.

According to legend, the *Santa Casa* in Italy contains three original walls of the house where Mary lived in Nazareth. The tradition also affirms that angels (led by St. Michael) transported the walls to Italy after the Muslims invaded the Holy Land. (The Virgin of Loreto is the patron saint of aviators.) The chapel contains statues of Tomás de la Canal and his wife, who are interred there. The chapel is only open to the public on the Virgin's day (September 8).

The Feast of the Virgin of Loreto is also celebrated at the little chapel of Loreto (*La Ermita*) on the corner of the Salida a Querétaro and the Cuesta de Loreto.

September 8: At 10 a.m. a civic ceremony takes place in the Jardín. The deaths of two citizens of San Miguel, Colonel Lucas Balderas and Colonel Gregorio Vicente Gelaty, in the Battle of Molino del Rey in 1848, is commemorated with the laying of a floral wreath in front of the old City Hall, as well as an honor guard and the lowering of the flag to half-staff. At 6 p.m. the flag on the roof of City Hall is lowered while the musical band of the Dragones de la Reina plays.

September 12: Commemoration of the heroic stand of the St. Patrick's Battalion in 1847 at the Battle of Churubusco. Flags are flown at half-staff.

September 13: *Homenaje a los Niños Héroes de Chapultepec* (Homage to the Boy Heroes of Chapultepec). Civic events in Parque Benito Juárez honor the six cadets who in 1847 during the American invasion of Mexico leapt to their death instead of surrendering. Flags are flown at half-staff.

September 14: Mass is offered for *Día de los Charros* (Horseman's Day) at the *Lienzo Charro* near *Unidad Deportiva*, the sports complex a few miles south on the road to Celaya.

Around 1 p.m. the *Cabalgata de los Conspiradores* begins. Horse riders arrive in the Jardín from Querétaro, re-enacting the messenger's ride from Querétaro to San Miguel in 1810.

September 15: The festivities for the Independence celebrations begin early in the evening. A torch is delivered by a marathon runner, from Querétaro to San Miguel, symbolizing the delivery of the message from *La Corregidora*.

At 11 p.m. the *Grito* is delivered by the mayor from the balcony of the Allende House, now the *Museo Histórico*. Thousands of people attend the emotional event. After the *Grito*, fireworks are lit in front of the Parroquia.

September 16: *Día de la Independencia de México* (Mexican Independence Day) is an official holiday. The day begins with civic acts and a wreath-laying ceremony at the *Museo Histórico*.

At 11 a.m. a military parade begins on the Ancha de San Antonio and wends its way via Zacateros, Canal, Hernández Macías, and Mesones to the Jardín.

At 6 p.m. a flag ceremony is held in front of the *ex-Presidencia* building opposite the Jardín.

At 6:15 p.m. the arrival of the Insurgents is re-enacted with a parade that begins on the Avenida Independencia and makes its way via Insurgentes, Hernández Macías, and Canal to the Jardín. The Independence Route Horse Ride ends up in front of the ex-Presidencia.

Fireworks begin at 9 p.m. Flags are flown at full-staff.

September 27: *Festividad de San Vicente de Paúl* (Feast of St. Vincent de Paul). The Franciscan priest is honored at the church and convent of La Concepción (Las Monjas).

September 27: Anniversary of the Attainment of Independence in 1821. The end of the War of Independence is commemorated. At 10 a.m. a civic ceremony commemorates the events. Flags are flown at full-staff.

September 28: Homage is paid to Juan José de los Reyes Martínez, "*El Pípila*," a native son, who on this date in 1810 burned down the door of the granary in Guanajuato. A small ceremony is conducted in the Jardín. A wreath is laid in front of his house on Barranca 44.

September 29: *Día de San Miguel Arcángel* (Feast Day of St. Michael the Archangel). San Miguel's patron saint's day takes place on this date if it falls on a Saturday; otherwise it is postponed until the following weekend, so the celebration sometimes occurs in early October. (See page 199.)

September 29: The feast day of San Miguel Arcángel is also celebrated at the chapel in the village of San Miguel Viejo, a few miles west of town.

September 30: Anniversary of the birth of Father José María Morelos y Pavón, a leader in the War of Independence, in 1765. At 10 a.m. a civic commemorative ceremony is conducted in the Jardín. Flags are flown at full-staff.

October
Movable events:

Last two weeks: The Cervantino Festival, one of the most important cultural events in Latin America, is held in Guanajuato, but some of the concerts and events take place in San Miguel (www.festivalcervantino.gob.mx).

Last Sunday: In Mexico Daylight Savings Time ends at 2 a.m. Clocks are set back one hour.

October 4: *Festividad de San Francisco de Asis* (Feast Day of St. Francis of Assisi). The founder of the Franciscan Order is honored at the San Francisco Church with fireworks and a Mass.

October 7: Anniversary of the death of Senator Belisario Domínguez in 1913. The senator gave a speech in the Senate against President Victoriano Huerta, for which he was murdered. Mexico's Medal of Honor is named after him. Flags are flown at half- staff.

October 12: *Día de la Raza* (Day of the Race, Columbus Day). Anniversary of the Discovery of America in 1492. There is a statue of Christopher Columbus (Cristóbal Colón) on the corner of Calle Benito Juárez and Calle San Francisco where at 10 a.m. a civic ceremony is conducted. Flags are flown at full-staff.

October 22: *Aniversario de la Constitución del Ejército Insurgente Libertador* (Anniversary of the Constitution of the Liberating Army) in 1810. Flags are flown at full-staff.

October 23: *Día Nacional de la Aviación* (National Aviation Day). Flags are flown at full-staff.

October 24: United Nations Day. Flags are flown at full-staff.

October 27: *Día de los Huerfanitos* (Day of the Little Orphans). Some of the customs relating to the Day of the Dead ceremonies are observed. Souls with no living relatives are received by the community with bread and water hung on doors.
October 28: *Día de los Accidentados*. Souls who died in accidents or violent deaths are remembered.
October 30: Anniversary of the birth of Francisco I. Madero, president of Mexico from 1911-1913, in 1873. Flags are flown at full-staff.
October 30: *Día de los Niños Limbos* (Day of the Children in Limbo) is dedicated to the souls of children who died in childbirth before baptism.
October 31: *Día de los Angelitos* (Day of the Little Angels) is dedicated to the souls of children who died in infancy, but were baptized and are thus free of sin.

November
Movable Events:

Third Monday: Although the anniversary of the start of the Mexican Revolution (El Aniversario de la Revolución Mexicana) is actually on November 20, it is celebrated on the third Monday in order for citizens to enjoy a long weekend. This is a legal holiday, but parades and fireworks still take place on November 20.

Fourth Thursday: Thanksgiving Holiday in the U.S.

Last Week: The International Festival of Jazz and Blues.

Last Two Weeks: *Feria Nacional de la Lana y el Latón* (The National Wool and Brass Fair) is held at the Plaza Cívica.

November 1: *Día de todos los Santos* (All Saints' Day) honors every saint, known or unknown.

The Day of the Dead (*Día de los Muertos*) is probably the most colorful and curious of Mexican traditions. On November 1, *Día de Todos los Santos* (All Saints' Day), and *Día de los Fieles Difuntos* (All Souls' Day), November 2, families unite to remember their deceased loved ones. The ancient Aztecs considered death the beginning of life, and believed that all souls lived on and returned to earth one day each year, seeking nourishment, community, and remembrance.

The first day is for all saints and the angelitos, the little angels, deceased children, and the second for adults. The grieving process is transformed into a celebration of life with the construction of beautiful altars and the preparation of food, drink, bright decorations, and memorabilia of the departed, called *ofrendas*.

As in many parts of Mexico, in San Miguel de Allende altars are set up not only in private homes but also in public spaces including stores, offices, and markets. Altars are created around the Jardín, the Biblioteca Pública, the Instituto Allende, the Museo Histórico, and the historic San Juan de Dios Cemetery on Calle San Antonio Abad, known as the Panteón Viejo which was opened to the public in 2008 after being closed (and neglected) for 50 years. The cemetery was built in 1782 by Father Joaquin Hidalgo y Costilla, brother of Miguel Hidalgo.

Thousands of people gather at the *Panteón Guadalupe* cemetery, located on a narrow street that parallels the Salida a Celaya, from early morning to nightfall, cleaning grave sites, arranging flowers, and decorating the graves with personal belongings and photographs of the deceased, as well as food and drink.

November 2: *Día de los Fieles Difuntos* (All Souls' Day), better known as the Day of the Dead. It is an unofficial holiday, with most businesses and many stores closed for all or part of the day. This is the only day that the crypt underneath the Parroquia is open to the public.

November 6: Commemoration of the Promulgation of the National Independence Act by the Congress of Chilpancinco in 1913. Flags are flown at full-staff.

November 12: *Día del Cartero* (Day of the Mailman). All post offices in Mexico are closed.

November 20: *Día de la Revolución Mexicana* celebrates the beginning of the Mexican Revolution, in 1910. At 10 a.m. a civic ceremony takes place along with a parade. Fireworks at night. (It is a legal holiday on the third Monday, see above.)

November 22: *Festividad de Santa Cecilia* (Feast of St. Cecilia), honoring the patron saint of the blind and musicians. The celebrations start the night before, with musicians serenading the saint in front of the Templo de la Salud on the Plaza Cívica.

November 23: *Día de la Armada de México* (Mexico's Day of the Fleet). Flags are flown at full-staff.

December:
Movable Events:

   Last two weeks: *Festival de San Miguel de Allende*, a chamber music festival (www.festivalsma.com).

December 3: The *novena* of the *Virgen de Guadalupe* begins nine days of prayers, Masses, and fireworks, especially in colonia Guadalupe and culminates at the fiesta in her honor on December 12. (See entry below.) Fireworks nightly.

December 8: *Festividad de la Inmaculada Concepción* (Feast of the Immaculate Conception) is celebrated at La Concepción Church (Las Monjas) and at the Santa Casa in the Oratorio. The Virgin Mary once was one of the town's six patron saints.

December 11: At 11 p.m. a Mariachi Mass is celebrated at the San Francisco church.

December 12: *Día de la Virgen de Guadalupe* (Feast of the Virgin of Guadalupe), Mexico's Patroness, Queen of Heaven, Empress of the Americas, Queen of Mexico, once was also one of San Miguel's patron saints. (There is even an official website: www.virgendeguadalupe.org.mx.)

In late 1531 a peasant named Juan Diego had a vision of the Virgin and told a local prelate, who demanded proof. The story goes that the Virgin again appeared to the Indian and told him to gather roses, not a promising enterprise, considering it was December. Nevertheless, he found them, cut them, and wrapped them in his cloak, a *tilma*, and presented them to the gathered priests. The life-sized figure of the Virgin had appeared on the cloth. It hangs today in the Basílica in Mexico City. In the middle of the 18th century Pope Benedict XIV proclaimed her Patron of New Spain. She is often referred to as *La Morenita* (The Little Dark-skinned One). Juan Diego was canonized in 2002. Octavio Paz wrote: "The Mexican people, after more than two centuries of experiments, have faith only in the Virgin of Guadalupe and the National Lottery."

At 9 a.m. there begins a *perigrinación* from the *Puente de los Frailes* (the Bridge of the Friars), about four miles south of the city on the road to Celaya. Hundreds of people participate, among them many cowboys. The procession ends up around noon for a Mass at the Parroquia de San Antonio de Padua.

Celebrations also take place in the Jardín, at the San Juan de Dios market, and the Ignacio Ramírez market. There are dancers and mariachi bands. A big fiesta takes place at the church in Colonia Guadalupe.

At 5 p.m. a procession leaves *La Ermita* chapel on the Salida a Querétaro and moves to Calle San Francisco and thence to the Oratorio where a Mass is celebrated.

Fireworks in front of the Parroquia follow soon after dark.

December 16-24: Nine *Posadas*. "*Posada*" means "inn" in Spanish. December 16 marks the beginning of the Posadas, held for nine evenings before Christmas, reenacting the search by Mary and Joseph to find a place at an inn in order to give birth to Jesus.

In some neighborhoods simple candlelit processions reenact the search. Each night a different home offers food and drink. Some neighborhoods feature floats with *mojigangas* (large *papier mâché* puppets). In others there is caroling, the breaking of a *piñata*, and children in costumes. Sometimes two children, dressed as Joseph and Mary, ride a burro through the streets, while other children dress up as angels.

The *Posadas* start out from a different church (see entry below) each evening at 7 p.m.

December 16: The first *posada* leaves from the Parroquia, follows Correo, Murillo, Núñez, Calzada de la Presa, Acamapixtli, Homobono, Puente de Umarán, Colegio, Mesones, and ends at the Templo de la Salud on the Plaza Cívica.

December 17: The second *posada* leaves from the Templo de la Salud on the Plaza Cívica, then follows Mesones, Hernández Macías, Calzada de la Luz, Loreto, Insurgentes, and ends at the Santa Ana Church.

December 18: The third *posada* leaves from the Santa Ana church on Insurgentes, then follows Hidalgo, Canal, Zacateros, Ancha de San Antonio, Orizaba, 28 de Abril, Tinajitas, and ends at the Parroquia de San Antonio.

December 19: The fourth *posada* leaves the Parroquia de San Antonio, then follows the Callejón de San Antonio, Ancha de San Antonio, Codo, Tenerías, Terraplén, Sollano, Correo, Corregidora, and ends at the San Francisco Church.

December 20: The fifth *posada* leaves from the San Francisco church, then follows Corregidora, Recreo, Hospicio, Cuadrante, Hernández Macías, Canal, Beneficencia, San Rafael, and ends at the San Juan de Dios church.

December 21: The sixth *posada* leaves from the San Juan de Dios church on San Rafael, then follows San Antonio Abad, Canal, crosses the Guanajuato Bridge, then follows Avenida Guadalupe, Insurgentes, and ends at the Oratorio.

December 22: Anniversary of the death of José María Morelos y Pavón in 1815 during the War of Independence. Flags are flown at half-staff.

December 22: The seventh *posada* leaves from the Oratorio, then follows Pepe Llanos, Juárez, San Francisco, Reloj, Calzada de la Luz, Calzada de la Aurora, and ends in *La Herradura* (a small square in Colonia Aurora).

December 23: The eighth *posada* leaves from Calzada de la Aurora, then follows Colegio Militar, Francisco González Bocanegra, Volanteros, Quebrada, Umarán, Zacateros, and ends at La Concepción church (Las Monjas).

December 24: Christmas Eve, called *Nochebuena*. The ninth and last *posada* begins at Las Monjas church and end at the Parroquia de San Miguel.

Mass is celebrated throughout the day in many churches.

December 25: *Día de Navidad* (Christmas Day) is a legal holiday.

December 28: *Día de los Santos Inocentes* (Holy Innocents' Day), Mexico's version of April Fool's Day, is celebrated with practical jokes and lots of teasing.

Throughout the day and evening children gather in the Jardín armed with eggshells filled with flour and confetti. They chase each other with cheerful abundance around the plaza, cracking the *cascarones* on the heads of unsuspecting friends and passers-by.

December 29: Anniversary of the birth of Venustiano Carranza in 1859. Carranza was twice president of Mexico during the revolutionary period, in 1914 and again from 1915-1920. Flags are flown at full-staff.

December 31: New Year's Eve. Mass is celebrated at many churches during the day. A midnight Mass is celebrated at several churches. The town is crowded. Fireworks erupt, often long before midnight. When the clock strikes twelve, some San Miguel residents eat one grape with each sounding of the church bells, signifying, one hopes, fruitfulness and plenty for the coming year.

Bibliography

Some interesting information and pleasant reading about San Miguel de Allende, in English and Spanish.

Behind the Doors of San Miguel de Allende. Robert de Gast. Petaluma, Ca.: Pomegranate, 2000.

Breve historia de Guanajuato. Mónica Blanco, et al. México, D.F.: El Colegio de México, 2000.

Descripción de la Villa de San Miguel el Grande y su Alcaldía Mayor, 1777. Juan Benito Díaz de Gamarra. San Miguel de Allende, Gto.: Amigos de San Miguel, 1994.

Cossio del Pomar in San Miguel de Allende. Maline Gilbert McCalla, translator. Querétaro: ImpreColor, 2007.

Diario de un viaje a la Nueva España. Francisco Ajofrín. México, D.F.: Secretaria de Educación Pública, 1986.

El Agua en San Miguel de Allende, ayer, hoy y mañana. Enrique García y García. San Miguel de Allende, Gto.: PTF S.C., 2006.

Estampas Sanmiguelenses 3. José Cornelio López Espinoza. San Miguel: Presidencia Municipal, 2006.

Fiesta y Tradición en San Miguel de Allende. Beatriz Cervantes Jáuregui y Ana María Crespo. Guanajuato, Gto.: Instituto Estatal de la Cultura de Guanajuato, 1999.

Flores Silvestres de San Miguel de Allende, A Pocket Guide to the Wild Flowers of San Miguel. Richard Cretcher. San Miguel de Allende, Gto.: R&D Publishing, 2006. (Spanish and English)

Guía del Turista. Miguel J. Malo y León de Vivero. n.d. (Spanish and English)

Nothing to Declare. Mary Morris. New York: Penguin Books, 1988.

On Mexican Time: A New Life in San Miguel. Tony Cohan. New York: Broadway Books, 2000.

Paseos Culturales en San Miguel de Allende. Luis Felipe Nieto Gamiño. Consejo de Turismo, n.d. (Spanish and English)

Perfil de una Villa Criolla, San Miguel de Allende 1555-1810. Rosalia Aguilar. México, D.F., 1986.

San Miguel and the War of Independence. Mamie Spiegel. Self-published, 2005.

San Miguel de Allende. Tom Scott and Stirling Dickinson. Brandenburgh Press, 1969.

San Miguel de Allende. Robert Somerlott. San Miguel de Allende, Gto.: Biblioteca Pública, 1991.

San Miguel de Allende: Cruce de Caminos. León, Gto.: Impresos ABC, 2006.

San Miguel de Allende: Guia del Visitante. Rosalia Aguilar, et al. México, D.F.: PC Editorial, 1993.

San Miguel Allende, Official Guide. I.N.A.H. México, D.F., 1968.

San Miguel de Allende, su historia, sus monumentos. Francisco de la Maza. México, D.F.: Frente de Afirmación Hispanista, A.C., 1972.

Sliced Iguana. Isabella Tree. London: I.B. Tauris and Co., 2008.

Some Common and Interesting Plants of San Miguel de Allende. John and Anne Parker. Edmonton, Alberta: Plant Press Publications, 1999.

The Churches and Chapels of San Miguel de Allende. Robert de Gast. Birdsnest, Va.: E&R Publishing, 1998.

The Doors of San Miguel de Allende. Robert de Gast. Petaluma, Ca.: Pomegranate, 1995.

Un Paseo Por San Miguel de Allende. Artes de México No. 139, n.d.

Wild & Wonderful: Nature up Close in the Botanical Garden 'El Charco del Ingenio', San Miguel de Allende. Walter L. Meagher and Wayne Colony. San Miguel de Allende, Gto.: W&W Publishing, 2008.

Acknowledgments

Many people helped make this book possible by providing advice, information, encouragement, and support. I thank them all.

David Ashton, Robert Baines, Fernando Banca, Marcela Cash, Evelyn Chisolm, Dorothy Cretcher, Richard Cretcher, Mariana Ferreiro Braun, Wayne Colony, Rogelio Flores, Kelvia Ford, Wayne Ford, Norberto Godínez, Juan Gómez, Primitivo González, Howard Haynes, Jesús Ibarra, Miguel Kegel, Betty Kempe, Al Kocourek, Michael Long, Robin Loving Rowland, Mario Mendoza, Marie Moebius, Julieta Moreno, Bill Munro, Clay Primrose, Ken Rowland, Sylvia Samuelson, Lynne Slattery, John Stevenson, Mary Sweatland, Regina Thomas von Bohlen, Saturnino Tovar, Alexander Trapp, Héctor Ulloa.